PRAISE

"Travis Apple is the perfect person to write this book because his career success personifies the title. In my 45 plus years in the Sports and Entertainment industry, encompassing a decade teaching as a University Professor and three plus decades operating as a Senior Executive at iconic sports properties, I have never seen anyone with the work rate, the ability to create relationships or produce the conversion/ success rate of Travis. Truly a 'coaches son' he exemplified getting in early, hustling all day including working through lunch and staying late while being totally focused on producing results. His 'Root' stats (call volume, call duration, appointments set and referrals) were invariably double the next best producer. Not surprisingly his 'Fruit' stats (tickets sold, revenue produced and average revenue per sale) were also double the next best performer. In short, he truly lived it, taught it as a Leader and is now sharing 'Next Practices' (Future Best Practices) for the world to learn from the Best!"

DR. BERNIE MULLIN, Founder and Chairman of
The Aspire Sports Marketing Group

"Not surprisingly, Travis has written a must-read for anyone looking to have success in Sports Sales. This is the playbook that Travis personally followed which has led to his, and many others, success in our industry."

LOU DEPAOLI, EVP & CRO at New York Mets

"From the moment we met, Travis was fully committed to success. And not in a lip-service type of way, I mean he was ALL-IN.

Some people are nouns, others are verbs, and unequivocally Travis is a verb who is all about action and implementation. His commitment to success is unmatched"

COREY BRETON, CRO Global Attractions at Legends

"The grind, the hustle, the countless objections...that's just sales to most people. To Travis, it's fuel. It's an opportunity to learn, but also to teach. Travis has built a stellar reputation as one of the best sales leaders and trainers in our business. *Hustle Your Way to Success in Sports Sales* is a sneak peek into what it takes to be successful, but also to develop the calluses to survive in the sports business as a seller. Congratulations on taking this step to invest in yourself to learn from the best."

RAVEN JEMISON, Vice President, Team Marketing Business Operations of the NBA, G-League, and WNBA

"Travis has a wealth of experience in the industry combined with a history of finding talented young men and women with potential and helping them on their journey. I can't think of better Sherpa to help you on your journey."

DR. BILL SUTTON, Founder and Principal of Bill Sutton & Associates

"Travis Apple's experience and approach to the Sports Industry provides a level of credibility and perspective that will make this book one of the more valuable reads. His passion, work ethic, intellectual curiousity and positive outlook on our industry has always provided Travis with an inside track to success. He has always been at or near the top in everything he does and will continue to be for quite some time. Travis has always outworked the situation and that has provided him with incredible insights and results to prove his approach. The Sports Industry gets better ever today because of people like Travis."

Nic Barlage, President of Business Operations at Cleveland Cavaliers

HUSTLE

YOUR WAY TO

$UCCE$$ IN

SPORTS

SALES

Playbook to **BEING ELITE** in the
SPORTS BUSINESS INDUSTRY

TRAVIS APPLE

Published & distributed by:
Sports Career Press
Indianapolis, Indiana

ISBN 978-1-7356108-0-1
First Edition
Printed in the United States of America

Book design and typesetting by Stewart A. Williams

CONTENTS

FOREWORD

One of my first memories of Travis Apple was in the Summer of 2007 when he was one of our Inside Sales representatives with the Atlanta Hawks and Atlanta Thrashers. He made his first big season ticket sale and as we talked through the process of getting the deal done at the top of the club level at Philips Arena, I could tell this young man was very talented. I had already seen the tireless work ethic and the drive to create success for himself, but he was now taking his game to a different level. Fast forward over a decade later I have seen him grow from that twenty-two-year-old with lofty career goals to one of the top revenue generation leaders in the sports industry. He has made a lifelong, positive impact on so many individuals personal and professional lives (mine included) that his presence in the industry is immeasurable.

When he told me, he was writing this book my initial reaction was "Why do you want give away all of your secrets?" Then I realized he has already been doing that for years by mentoring and growing the people he was encountering on a daily basis.

This book will allow a much larger audience to get the benefit of learning what it takes to be successful in the sports sales business from one of the best. Anyone, regardless of what point they are in their career will benefit from reading this book and utilizing the concepts it details. From someone thinking about entering the business as an inside sales rep to someone leading their own team.

After almost 15 years of being able to call Travis a teammate (on two occasions), a mentor, a motivator, and most importantly a good friend I am proud of what he has been able to do by creating this book that I know will help to only add to the impact he has had on our industry.

—*Chris Zaber*

INTRODUCTION

When I was in sixth grade, money was just as important to me as it is now. The school fundraiser that year was a magazine subscription drive, and the prize for the individual with the most sales at the end piqued my interest. He or she would be able to enter in the money machine for one minute to grab as much dough as they could. Money was all the motivation I needed.

I started with my parents. I quickly talked them into to adding some new subscriptions for themselves, as well as Kid's Sports Illustrated for me. (I loved the cards and poster that came with each edition.) I then moved to my grandparents, aunts, uncles, and cousins. Then I started cold-calling. Yes, even when I was 12 years old, I was making cold calls and loving it. These weren't really "calls" exactly, but the effect was the same. I would jump on my Huffy Bike and ride door-to-door around the neighborhood of Delphos, Ohio (7,000 total people). Several of my classmates lived in the same area, so I had to get to my neighbors before they did.

After 3 weeks of selling magazines, I came out on top and was able to test my skills in the money machine. After a minute of wind and dirty money hitting me in the face,

I walked away with $27 and a huge smile on my face. I had accomplished my goal; I was the top salesperson and I made "free" money.

Looking back, I realize selling magazines door-to-door is very similar to selling tickets for a professional franchise. A successful sales representative needs to have a competitive edge and must always want to be #1. They need to be a little greedy (which is not a bad word).

Growing up living in a household where my father played college baseball, coached high school baseball, and was a school's athletic director, I didn't have much choice but to play sports. Fortunately for me, that is exactly what I wanted to do. Playing sports professionally—it didn't really matter which sport—was my passion and my dream.

Flash forward to high school: at 5'10" and a 160 pounds soaking wet, it was going to be a long stretch to make into the big leagues in any sport. So I had to change my goals a bit. If I wasn't going to be *playing* sports, I at least needed to work for a professional sports team. I started writing for the local newspaper, the *Delphos Herald*. I wrote articles about the local high school sports teams, as well as preview articles and much more for the daily paper. This was my first experience in multi-tasking, as I would go to school from 8am – 3pm, head to practice, spend evening covering a sporting event and writing an article on the local teams, then go to bed and start all over again the next day. It was worth it, though, as every other Friday I would get a check. As a 17-year-old senior in high school, I was making more money than I would have ever dreamed. I loved it.

When it came time to choose a college, I thought about

picking a school close to Delphos so I could continue to live with my parents, work at the newspaper, and hang out with my friends. However, that wasn't going to get me to where I ultimately wanted to go in life. I needed to find a school that I could stay on campus, build new relationships, and hopefully—after 4 years of paying a lot of money to attend—help me get the job I wanted.

I ended up choosing Ashland University, a small Division II school in the middle of rural Ohio. My main reason for attending Ashland was that it offered a major in sports communication, which allowed me to get hands on with the TV broadcasts as well as writing articles for the college newspaper. From my freshmen year, I was able to get on-air experience; I did play-by-play for the football and men's and women's basketball games. We also had a weekly sports show called Gametime Situation (check it out on YouTube) and I began writing for the college newspaper. By my junior year I was the Sports Director for the campus TV station and the Sports Editor of *The Collegian*. Both of these jobs gave me my first experience of managing other people.

Throughout college, I transitioned into grabbing a few other majors in Journalism and Electronic Media Production (still no sales or marketing major). I was having a blast working with my friends and doing and saying whatever I wanted on TV. Most colleges require students to get real life experience with an internship, but I decided to go above and beyond and get 5 of them while I was in college. I worked for a local TV station, two local newspapers, a local hardware store, and the Mansfield Motorsports Speedway, which eventually changed my career path forever. I knew absolutely nothing about racing, but it seemed like a really cool gig. I would work every weekend at the local events helping out with the PA Announcing, writing press releases, and any other assignment that needed done. I literally spent every Friday, Saturday, and Sunday at the racetrack, including several weekends where I actually slept in the suites.

After working at the racetrack for 3 weeks, the owner asked me to work full-time Monday thru Friday in addition the weekend races. My responsibilities immediately increased as I helped with the ticket sales, loading the concessions, answering phones, etc. About 3 weeks into working full time for $6 an hour, the General Manager came to me and asked if I would be interested in making more money? *What a stupid question*, I thought. *Who doesn't want more money?* He asked me to start selling trackside banners for $1,000 a piece, and I happily agreed. I had no idea what I was doing, but I opened up the Yellow Book and starting cold calling businesses. I had absolutely no training and no script, but regardless I was able to set a few appointments. I then started going door to door to businesses, and quickly I started having a lot of success. For every banner I sold, I was making 10% commission. I wasn't a math major, but I knew that was getting me $100 bucks in my pocket (or 10 cases of Keystone for my friends and I). From that moment forward, I knew that sales was what I wanted to do. I could control my own destiny and make as much money as I wanted.

After graduation, I started applying for jobs through multiple online sports websites, but I kept striking out. I received a few calls back with door-to-door sales, but nothing to write home about. I started to feel like I was destined to end up back at my parents' house working for the *Delphos Herald*. (No offense to the paper, but it just wasn't something I wanted to do again.) So I made one last attempt; I had a connection that lived in Atlanta, who in turn had a connection with the Atlanta Hawks and Thrashers. I emailed this person, and she gave me the email of the individual to send my resume to. I got a bit anxious when I didn't hear back from anyone after a day, so I decided to look the manager up and call directly and left a message. Shortly thereafter I had my first real phone interview with Corey Breton, the Inside Sales Manager for both teams.

Throughout this book, you will read a lot about going above and beyond the call of duty. When interviewing, this is another time you need to do just that. After the short phone interview, I immediately sent a thank-you card to Corey and a follow up email asking him what I could do better in the interview process. A few days later on a Wednesday afternoon, Corey followed up with me and said he would like me to come to Atlanta for a face to face interview. I immediately told him I would be down on Friday (not really thinking that was only 2 days away). I knew I couldn't afford a plane ticket, so I decided to make the 12-hour drive to Atlanta.

I was fortunate enough on that Friday to meet several of my most influential mentors to this day. I interviewed with Corey, Brendan Donohue, and Chris Zaber as well as several representatives of the Hawks and Thrashers. On Saturday, I attended a Thrashers game, and Corey came to me after the first period and offered me the job. I was ecstatic. The drive back was awesome as I thought about the new life I'd be starting in a few short months…as an adult in the real world. It was a big adjustment, but what I learned quickly is that the sports sales business is a grind and the key to success is hustle.

From that day on I have immersed myself in the sports business and have really enjoyed my journey throughout. In my career, I went on to work for the Pittsburgh Pirates, Orlando Magic, Phoenix Suns/Mercury, NBA League Office, and the Miami Marlins. I have been very fortunate to work with a lot of great people, hired and trained a bunch of very successful individuals, lived in great cities, and have made long lasting friends.

For those of you that know me, hustle has always been a big part of my life and certainly a big part of my career. I learned early on in both that the most talented athletes or the better sales people don't always end up being the best or at number one on the sales board. It all comes down to control what you can control and effort is a key factor in that. Good things happen to good people that put themselves in a good position.

Sales is a numbers game; the more hustle and effort you put in the better off you will be. By picking up this book, that is a step in you taking to better yourself. You will see a constant theme in the book and that is effort and motivation will lead you to be successful. Can you make more calls, set more appointments, get in front of more people than the next to be highly successful, and gain more referrals? In my opinion, it's not about being good or great; it's about finding a way to be an elite sales professional. Hustlers in this business are laser focused, dream big, not afraid to take a risk, never quit, think outside the box, create their own path, and most importantly never quit.

My entire life has been about hustle and early on in my career I was provided the below talking points on hustle.

- **Hustle** is doing something that everyone is absolutely certain can't be done.
- **Hustle** is getting a commitment because you got there first or stayed with it after everyone else gave up.
- **Hustle** is shoe leather and elbow grease and sweat and missing lunch.
- **Hustle** is getting prospects to say, "yes" after they've said "no" twenty times.
- **Hustle** is doing more unto a customer than the other guy can do unto him.
- **Hustle** is believing in yourself and the business you're in.
- **Hustle** is the sheer joy of winning.
- **Hustle** is being the sorest loser in town.
- **Hustle** is hating to take vacation because you might miss a piece of action.
- **Hustle** is heaven if you're a hustler.
- **Hustle** is hell if you're not.

If you look up the definition of hustler; it will tell you that it is an individual that is determined to succeed and a go-getter. If you don't know already, you will quickly find out this business is not a 9 to 5 job. If you look at it as a job, then you should do something else as you will quickly be worn out. To be elite in this business, you need to invest in yourself and be ready to hustle even when it's not working hours. By picking up this book; you are already hustling and starting to put yourself in a position to be successful. My hope is that you are reading this book as a student in college looking to get into this industry or someone that is already in this industry that is trying to be elite. My hope is that you will continue to go back and read several of the chapters a few more times as you build your career in this great industry. Each chapter is divided into easily accessible pieces, so you can quickly go back and reread scripts, examples, and takeaways to continue to apply them to your day. Within each chapter, I lay out three key takeaways for each section that will hopefully help you internalize the lessons and apply them to your career.

Please enjoy this book and hopefully you can take something out of it, and it will help you get into the beast of the business side of the sports industry. Feel free to reach out to me on LinkedIn at any time as I would love to connect further. Throughout the book, you will see many different types of scripts and information provided to help you be successful. Much of this information was around way before I started in the business and will be around long after I leave but I will tell you one thing, it works! But it only works if you HUSTLE! Again, this is all in my opinion but hopefully it helps! Best of luck!

—*Travis Apple*

CHAPTER 1

PREPARING FOR SUCCESS

After landing my first job, I have been fortunate to never have to go through the process of applying for jobs. When you hustle and succeed in this business, opportunities will present themselves. However, even when opportunities came across my plate, I still always had to be prepared and ready to go, as this industry is very competitive. Each and every day you will need to continue to prepare for success and your future. To use a baseball analogy, it's all about being ready in the bullpen to get that call that you are now in the game. Guess what: you won't even get a chance to be on the bench or have that opportunity if you don't practice. Even if you are already in this business, you need to ensure that you are continuing to evolve and continuing to prepare for success.

BUILDING YOUR RESUME

Many times, getting an interview for a job opportunity is the hardest part of the process. As you browse all of the websites, go to Career Fairs, and apply for every job that you are interested in; ask yourself are you doing anything to

1

differentiate yourself from the 1,000 other people that want that same job?

It all starts with your resume. Your resume is most likely the first time the hiring manager will see your name and examples of what you will bring to their team. In the years I have been in this business, I have seen a lot of resumes—unfortunately a lot more bad resumes than good ones.

When constructing your resume, make sure it looks the part. It needs to look professional because you are putting it in front of professionals, and you want to make sure it stands out .

Resume breakdown from top to bottom should look as follows:

- Name and all of your contact information
- Education
- Experience
- Activities
- Skills and Abilities

With the contact information, make sure you are putting all of your correct and current information on how a hiring manager can get a hold of you. It sounds simple, but you wouldn't believe how many times the address is no longer right or the number rings to the applicant's childhood home. Most importantly, make sure the email address you have on your resume is the one that you check on a regular basis. There is nothing worse than responding to an email that was sent 2 weeks ago. Remember, the hiring managers are hiring for a sales position; it is expected that you follow up right away. If you can't follow up with a hiring manager promptly, what makes them think you would do so with your customers?

The education part of your resume should be pretty simple. School name, type of degree, majors/minors, and your year of graduation. If you have a GPA that is worth bragging about, then include it; if not, it's better to leave it off. In the sports sales industry, GPA isn't very important. (Parents please don't kill me for saying this!) You don't have to be a rocket scientist to be successful in this career path.

The experience category is by far the most important on a resume. A hiring manager wants to see what the candidate did during school to differentiate themselves from everyone else. This is not a place to put what classes you took; every single student that graduated with the major/minor would have had to take the same exact classes. Hiring managers want to see that you have had experience in the real world and that you were willing to go above and beyond the call of duty—not just playing the video game *Call of Duty*, but actually taking the time to get yourself some real-life experience while in school.

What kind of experience should you get? As much as you can, as often as you can. Most colleges now require 1 internship in your 4 years. Why stop with just 1? Do you want to make your resume not only stand out but you as a candidate stand out? Show that you had 3-4 internships, that you job shadowed 3-4 different places, and that you are willing to do everything you can to make it in this industry. This may take you away from playing intramurals, hanging with friends, playing another game of beer pong, etc., but it's going to be very beneficial for you down the road.

Again, this industry is going to take a lot of long hours and dedication, and the hiring manager wants to see someone willing to do that.

As a hiring manager, the first part of the resume that I look at is the experience. I am going to favor a candidate that has some experience in the industry, not just flipping hamburgers. I want to see that the candidate has put some time and effort into finding what career is best for them.

As important as internships and job shadowing is for building out your resume, it's even more important to gain the real-life experience for yourself. Go out and get internships in sales, community relations, marketing, public relations, and anything else that you may have a little interest in. See what a good fit for you *before* you graduate and try to make it on your own. Another great thing about most internships is that you can bounce around a bit and learn other areas of the business. That way, when it comes to applying for jobs, you know exactly which ones you are most interested in.

Activities are also very important in showing off your resume. A hiring manager wants to know how you spend your free time and what other things you are interested in. Many of these activities could help you down the road when you are in a sales position, as you can then start reaching out to similar groups to the ones you were in and form a ticketing package for the specific groups. These activities can vary from Student Council, volunteer opportunities, intramurals, clubs, etc. Just get involved and get experience in anything and everything.

While you want to include as much experience as possible, don't ramble on your resume. Resumes shouldn't be over 1 page when you are just getting out of college. Unfortunately, you probably haven't done enough that is worth putting on your resume in your first 21 years of life. Remember: hiring managers have to look through 1,000 resumes. They don't have time to flip the page. Also, they are probably not going to take the time to read through every single word, so make sure that the important facts you want to get across stand out.

As you start building out your resume, get as much feedback as possible. Go to your Career Development Center for advice. Ask your internship supervisor to look it over. Ask your friends, family, or you can even email me your resume and I will provide you feedback. Building a perfect resume is the first step in having a career in the sports sales industry.

1. Research examples of resumes and ensure its professional.
2. Gain as much experience and internships as you can.
3. Short, sweet, and to the point.

BE SMART WITH SOCIAL MEDIA

If I would have written this book when I first got into this business in 2007, I probably wouldn't have needed to write anything about social media. Now, though, it is one of the most important ways we communicate who we are, both personally and professionally. I would have never thought a social media tool online would be a way to get in touch with decision makers or decision makers would view social media prior to making decisions.

You would be surprised how many people try to get into this business—or any business for that matter—without a

5

good grasp of their personal brand when it comes to social media. No matter if you are applying for your first job, if you are already working, or if you want a new job, it is crucial to look through all of your social media accounts and delete anything that is not going to help your brand. It seems to be inevitable that every year of the NFL Draft, a top prospect gets unwanted media attention because they had posted something stupid on a social media site years earlier. Think about how easy it is for a hiring manager to quickly search your name in any of the social media platforms and find each and every thing you posted.

My best piece of advice is to really focus on separating your personal social media from your professional ones. Be sure to make sure there is nothing on any platforms, though, that would make leaders ask questions. This could be as simple as a picture, a repost, or a comment that you made. Think about it from the hiring perspective; there are a lot of people that want this same job, so why would they want a candidate whose social media posts could reflect poorly on the company. I am not going to tell you to not have any personal social media, because I understand the value and benefit of putting yourself out there. What I would tell you, though, is that you should be smart with it and understand the strengths and potential harms that it could cause.

One of the best professional social media channels in my opinion is LinkedIn. Back in 2008, I started hearing about it and decided to sign up for LinkedIn with the mindset that I can talk about my accomplishments and maybe a recruiter will find me. The evolution of social media and specifically LinkedIn really starting ramping up a few years later. Today,

LinkedIn is an essential tool to grow your business. Even if you are looking for that first job, a career change, or you already have the position you want, your LinkedIn account can be utilized in similar fashion. We just talked about building your resume, which you can use to fill out your LinkedIn profile. I can tell you from experience that many hiring managers look at resumes and then immediately go check out social media, specifically LinkedIn.

As you build out your LinkedIn Profile or if you already have one, take a dive into it again to ensure that it has everything you need to be successful. Having a great LinkedIn page helps in many different ways, from getting hired to selling sports at a high level. Social selling really leverages your personal and professional brand to fill your pipeline with the right people and insights. Everything you put into your profile should be trying to catch the attention of a prospective hiring manager or customer; not for your friends to comment on how crazy the weekend was.

As you put in your headshot, take the time to either get a professional photo taken or at the very least wear your best clothes and take a nice picture with a blank background. No hiring manager wants to see you wearing your intramural shirt or a shirt you just played beer pong in. You would be surprised on how many LinkedIn profiles still don't have a professional headshot; this will help you stand out.

LinkedIn has provided the opportunity to put a background in your main profile page as well. If you are already working for a team, it is very easy to place a photo of their home venue. If you are looking for a job, think creatively on what that background may look like. It could be pictures of sales books, a sales quote, or a nice image of your college/university.

As you think about your headline or title, don't be generic. If you have a role, give your title and then say what you are going to do help potential customers that see your profile. For example: "Inside Sales Representative – Helping Clients Enjoy a Great Experience at [Venue]". If you are applying for a role, try something like this: "School Graduate – Looking to Increase Revenue for a Sports Team". You will hear me say a lot that you need to go above and beyond and find ways to differentiate yourself; do that in everything you do.

When editing your contact information, it might seem pretty self-explanatory but be sure to include a phone and email that you use consistently. You can also add links to different websites so if you have some websites that you are proud of; feel free to share.

In my opinion, the most important part of a LinkedIn page is the summary page. This is really where you can describe how you are going to help a customer or why a hiring manager should hire you. As you fill out your summary, think about it from the perspective of someone trying to determine if they want to do business with you or respond to your email or invitation. Here's a good example:

> "As a proud member of the teams' front office, I take great pride in building long lasting relationships with companies, organizations, and individuals across the cities area.
>
> I specialize in working with each individual client to create an amazing experience that has a

long-lasting impression on employees, customers, and family and friends at a game.

Many companies look at our seating as an excellent means for developing relationships with new and existing clients. They have also realized the added benefit of utilizing our seating as a forum to cultivate internal relationships as well.

For anyone interested in learning more about the team, please contact me at [personalized email].

I look forward to hearing from you."

This is a simple summary message that details out who you are, what you do, how you do it, and ultimately how you can help. If you are looking for a role, think creatively about your summary page and do something very similar that hits on who you are, what you have done, how you have been successful, and ultimately why it's going to make sense for someone to hire you.

LinkedIn also gives you the ability to add websites and links, so if you have some good links from projects or successes you have had it's always good to include them. On the team side, be sure to add links to the different sales websites.

Finally, one of the biggest opportunities that LinkedIn offers it the ability for you to be recommended. Think about how beneficial this can be as a hiring manager is looking at your profile and they see a recommendation from one of your current bosses or professors talking about your work ethic or production. Or if a customer is talking about how great of experience they have had dealing with you and you always went above and beyond for them. This is very easy to do, but I don't see a lot of people doing it on a consistent basis because they don't take the time to ask. Focus on your top 3 customers or your top 3 bosses/professors and ask them to write a recommendation for you right away.

LinkedIn and other social media channels can be important to the success of your career, but unfortunately people also allow them to be their downfall. Take the time to really dig into what has/is on your social media sites and focus on how you can use them as a business tool.

1. Focus on your personal and professional brand through social media
2. Create an AWESOME profile
3. Ask your top 3 customers/professors for a recommendation

CHAPTER 2

CHOOSING THE RIGHT JOB

After spending 2.5 years in Atlanta and being groomed for a leadership role, I decided to make the move to Major League Baseball and work for the Pittsburgh Pirates and was fortunate to work there with two of my biggest mentors (Lou DePaoli and Chris Zaber). This was my first leadership role and a huge opportunity for me to make an impact in a lot of future careers. At the Pirates, we changed up our interview process where it was no longer a few-hour interview but an all day interview where we took candidates through the day and life of successful sales member. Throughout that entire day, we were able to quickly identify the characteristics in people that we wanted to surround ourselves with. We looked for who was coachable and who was willing to get after it for 10 hours that day. As I look back in my time in Pittsburgh, I couldn't be more proud of the accomplishments we made and the people we brought through the organization that are now doing bigger and better things in our industry.

Now that you have the perfect resume and the right social media profile, it's time to identify which positions are most intriguing to you and what roles fit you best.

You wouldn't believe how often candidates literally apply for every job that is open within an organization. Don't do that to yourself; you hopefully have put enough time and effort into your life that you don't want to get a job just to say you have a job but then you end up hating it. In this chapter, I will show you how to find the right job for you—and how to get it.

CHARACTERISTICS OF SUCCESSFUL SALES PROFESSIONALS

Many people have asked me over the years, "What does it take to be successful in this business or what are you looking for in a person in this specific role?" So before we dive into figuring out what jobs to apply for, I want to take this time to detail out to you the most important traits for success in this industry. After each characteristic, there will be several questions that can be asked, or a hiring manager will look for to ensure that you have what they are looking for.

Passion

To be successful in any role in the sports sales industry, you need to have a passion for what you are doing. What job is going to put a smile on your face every time you wake up or talk about it? What type of role is going to make you want to keep pushing yourself? I look for someone that always has a smile on their face and is a positive influence on the people around them.

Can you think of a family member or friend that all they do is complain about their job? How annoying is it to hear them talk about "counting down the days until retirement?"? My guess is you know someone that thinks that. You are getting into the real world and specifically the sports business because you probably have interest in sports. Challenge yourself to continue to have that passion every single day.

Similar to playing sports, there are going to be times that it is hard, but your passion will keep you going. Keep a smile and keep remembering how exciting it is to get to work for a professional sports team.

- Why are you interested in working in sports?
- Why are you interested in working in sales?
- How does this role fit into your career growth?

Work Ethic

You wouldn't believe the amount of people that have told me that I should hire them because they are the hardest worker. Enough talking the talk. I want someone that is going to walk the walk.

Work ethic is not how hard you think you worked that day or how long you were in the office. Work ethic is a combination of putting the time into perfecting your craft, working smart, doing the tasks that you are supposed to be doing, and giving it 110% on a daily basis. The individual that works the hardest and smartest will typically be the person that is putting themselves in a perfect position to be successful.

Work ethic can show right from your resume. Were you the person that settled with 1 internship or did you go above and beyond and get 2-3? Were you winning the hustle contest consistently in your sales role? Individuals that have good work ethic will consistently be the ones that are ultimately given more responsibility, more leadership opportunities, and ultimately are the people first in line for promotions.

- What have you done in the past to separate yourself from competition?
- How do you plan on remaining competitive in this field?
- How will you remain positive and upbeat through difficult times?

Coachability

I am sure everyone along the way has had a coach or teacher of some sort. You have probably seen individuals cut from a team, kicked out of class, or even fired because they were not coachable. Successful salespeople need to be coachable as there is going to be a lot of information thrown at you to learn as well as different scripts and talking points that people need to work with.

Many people struggle with the term coachability, as everyone thinks they can listen/learn. That is great but like anything, can you put your money where your mouth is? Give real life examples of how you are coachable and how you have applied specific trainings/teachings.

We are in an ever-changing business that you always need to be coachable no matter what role you are in. Have an open mind, be open to change, and most importantly listen to what is being taught because somewhere along the way the manager has been successful doing the same things they are teaching.

- What role would you consider yourself on a team; a coach, captain, or star player?

- What type of work atmosphere and management do you thrive under?
- Can you think of an example of when you didn't know how to perform a task and how you overcame it?

Competitiveness

I would imagine that every single person reading this book and every person that wants to be in the sports industry is pretty competitive. I am sure at one point in time in your life, you have played a sport or been a part of a team that is competing to win or be #1. Nothing should change once you get in the sports industry either.

Sales is a very competitive industry. Typically the most successful people are not the ones that are content with being #2. As a competitive person, and more importantly a successful sales representative, you need to be that person that is going to do everything in their power (fairly) to be #1. Competitive people are never content not being the best at their position and you need to have a competitive mindset to be successful.

- Do you love to win or hate to lose?
- How have you handled not being #1 in the past?
- How well do you work under pressure?

Confidence

Every day in sales, you will have to show confidence when talking on the phone, meeting with customers, and asking for the sale. I promise you will never sell anything if you are not confident. I promise you won't sell anything if your pitch sounds like this: "I think this is the best fit and probably the best seats, I don't know; what do you think?"

There is a big difference in being confident and being cocky. Too many people think being confident is showing their swagger and thinking they are better than the next. Confidence is a lot about always being on top of your game and having faith in yourself that you can be the best.

- How would you define self-confidence?
- Do you think there is a difference between confidence and arrogance?
- How confident are you?

Commitment

Think about when you were growing up and you were playing a sport: what is something you typically did prior to playing any games? If you don't know the answer, think about one of the most famous lines from Allen Iverson: PRACTICE!!!

If you want to have a long successful career in this business, you need to be committed and you have to continue to evolve and practice every single day. This business can be a grind; many people get out of the business because they lack a commitment to their craft. How are you going to challenge yourself each and every day? What are you going to do to take it to the next level? Commitment to learning, growing, and developing every single day will ultimately take you to the next level in life and certainly in this business.

- If you don't get this job, what type of job would you be looking for?
- Have you ever quit anything before, and if so, why?
- What aspects of this job appeal to you the least?

Teamwork

If you were a coach of a sports team, how would you feel if you had a star player who didn't treat his teammates well? Do you think that team would succeed? The same holds true in the sales environment; nobody enjoys leading someone that doesn't play by the rules and thinks they can get away with anything.

Many of the best salespeople want to become leaders in their career. It's going to be very hard for someone to be a leader if they are constantly not leading by example as a sales team member. Be honest, be open-minded, find ways to build relationships with those that are around you. Teamwork makes the dream work.

- What type of role would you look to play with the group if you were to start next week?
- Say you've worked for us for 6 months and someone new starts, what role do you play with that person?
- What if someone next to you is having all this great success, how do you respond?

If you have all of the above traits, then you are likely to succeed in what can be a challenging industry.

1. Identify which characteristics you need to work on and put a plan together to improve.
2. Great leaders are always looking for the people that can grow the business and ultimately take their job.
3. Remember: this business is a marathon, not a sprint.

Applying

Once you have identified your strengths and chosen your path, it's time to start looking for your first job or your next role in this industry. As you are going through job boards, I want you to think about the following items:

➤ What are you passionate about?
  ▸ What is going to make you get up every morning with a smile on your face and you have the mindset that you can't wait to get to the office that day.
➤ What is the actual role?
  ▸ Please don't apply for a job just because it is your favorite team of all time.
➤ Where is the role located?
  ▸ Are you willing to relocate? Can you see yourself living in that specific city?
➤ Finally, when you picture yourself in 2-3 years; can you see yourself doing that specific role for that certain company?

As you go through the application process, you want to make sure you put your best foot forward for each application you submit. Don't just apply for every job out there. More importantly, you will want to be able to do some research and have a good idea of the questions you are going to ask and the answers you are going to provide for each specific role that you apply for. The worst feeling in the world is getting a call from a hiring manager and you don't even remember applying for the job.

Though experience is helpful, don't just apply for jobs to get interview experience. Many of the hiring managers know each other, and if you start just gaining "interview experience" the word will get out and it could keep you from ever getting a job. If you need help interviewing, go to your Career Development Center or ask internship supervisors, professors, supervisors, etc. for their advice.

There have been countless times that I have gone through a phone screen with candidates and at the end they ask me if they would have to relocate to the specific city? It sounds crazy and a rather stupid question, but it has been asked a lot. For 99% of sports sales roles, you will be expected to relocate to the specific city and work in their office. Don't rule out relocation too quickly, though. No matter where you grew up in the world, there are always different places out there that would be really cool to live in and experience. Many people come out of college and use the excuse that they don't have the money to relocate or want to stay in their same hometown where they feel comfortable. By no means am I saying any of those reasons are bad reasons, but my advice to each and every one of you is to get out and go and move away at least once in your life. You can always go "home," and more than likely your first job out of school will not be your last.

Over my career in this industry, I have lived in 6 really great cities, have met a ton of great people, and have visited a lot of other great places. Don't hold yourself back; there is a good possibility that you become a better sales professional by moving away. Why? Being successful in sales in putting yourself in uncomfortable situations and finding a way to thrive. If you are relocating, you are now moving to a brand new city where you probably don't know many people, you have to sign a lease to live, buy your own groceries, spend money on day to day activities, and most importantly can't necessarily rely on your family and friends that could provide you a lot more comfort. (Again, parents don't be mad at me for saying that. Think of the bright side—your kids could move to a really cool vacation spot for you!)

As you look to embark on a career in professional sports sales, don't worry about what your title is. Titles are one of the biggest misconceptions in our industry; unfortunately I feel that a lot of people—whether it be parents/professors/mentors—who are giving the wrong advice on this subject. Titles will come as you continue to grow your career and it really doesn't matter if you are an Inside Sales Representative or a New Business Development Member. You are doing the same job.

Likewise, don't focus too much on compensation. As you are starting in the sports sale's world, you are not going to have a high base salary and the majority of your income will come from commissions. I realize that you will have bills to pay and you want to live comfortably, but if you are smart with money you can make it work. If you have confidence in yourself and you are willing to put the time and effort into it, you will eventually make more money than you ever imagined. Most first year sports sales professionals will make between $30,000-$45,000 with the opportunity to make much more because most organizations do not have a cap on compensation

So, how do you find that first job? The perfect way to start is to check the online job application sites—Teamworkonline.com, jobsinsports.com, careersinsports.com, teams' websites, LinkedIn, etc.—so you can see what opportunities are out there. Should you apply through those sites? Absolutely. However, that is also how 1,000 other people are going to apply for the same opportunity. If your resume stands out enough to still get a call that way, then congratulations! However, as a hiring manager, I can tell you it is almost impossible to get through the thousands of resumes that entry-level candidates submit.

Knowing that you are applying for a sales job, think about as if you are a salesperson and you are doing everything you can to get in front of your customer. Would you just stop with an introductory email? I hope your answer is no, because when you are in sales you are never going to stop with just one call. You may have to call that decision maker ten times before even getting a meeting with them. The same process should be in place when it comes to trying to get an interview with the hiring manager.

Now that you have applied online like everyone else, what else can you do to differentiate yourself? I would start by going onto the team's website and the front office page and find out who exactly is the hiring manager. Once you find out who that is, do your best to get 15 minutes of their time. Listed below are a few examples of ways you should try to get in contact with the hiring manager:

➤ Email the hiring manager directly with your resume
  ▸ It should be very easy to find out what the master emails are for a company. Look at press releases, bio pages, or just simply call the main line and ask for the email address. If you haven't done so already, be sure to sign up for a LinkedIn page, as

this is a very easy way to not only get noticed but also to look up contact info.

➤ Call the hiring manager directly
   ▶ Maybe you don't have the hiring manager's direct phone number, but I guarantee you can find the general line and call and ask for him/her directly. (Before you make this call, make sure you practice what you are going to say whether you talk to the hiring manager directly or if you will need to leave a voicemail."
      ▷ "<HIRING MANAGER NAME>, this is <YOUR NAME> and I am calling in regard to the posting for <POSITION>. I realize in sales you have to go above and beyond the call of duty, and that is why I am calling you directly. I am confident that I can really help your sales team grow their business. I would love the opportunity to interview for the <POSITION>. Again, this is <YOUR NAME>, please call me at <YOUR PHONE NUMBER>, once again <YOUR NAME> at <YOUR PHONE NUMBER>."
   ▶ Is this going to get you a call back every time? No. However, as a current hiring manager, I am going to make sure I respond to each and every person who gets in touch with me in a unique way.
➤ Mail Resume and Information to Hiring Manager
   ▶ Print your resume off on nice paper, write a hand-written note, and snail mail it the company with the attention of the hiring manager. Throughout the book, you will hear me talk about hand-written

notes quite a bit, as they are very important. Do not just write up a generic letter and send it along. It takes a little extra effort and time, but it will go a long way as odds are the hiring manager will look at a hand-written note as a more genuine way to reach out.

► Follow up with a phone call after your mail your resume.

I always make a point to interview any candidate that is willing to go above and beyond and show that they are differentiating themselves. My guess is that most hiring managers are similar.

1. Apply for the position that you are most interested in.
2. Control what you can control.
3. Go above and beyond to get in front of the hiring manager.

INTERVIEWING

When the day comes that you have an interview—be it an initial phone screen or an in-person meeting—make sure you are prepared and ready to go. For your first interview out of college, this is probably the most nerve-racking experience you will have for a while. Don't act like this is just another test that you can go out to the bars all night and wake up the next morning and "wing" it. Even after you are in this business and you are planning for your next move, you need to be prepared.

Regardless of how the interview is conducted, you should approach it the same way. For example, dress the part. Don't have a phone screen in your pajamas; dress professionally as this will help you feel and sound professional on the phone. Sports Sales jobs are heavily driven by utilizing the phone, so even if it's just a call you need to be ready to go. Make sure your phone is charged, and make sure you are in a spot that is quiet and has good cell service. Don't use the excuse later that you aren't good at talking on the phone. If that's the case, you will need to find a new career path.

When it comes to a face-to-face interview, many teams will let you know that they would like to formally meet you but you will have to provide your own transportation. I know this is a touchy subject, but this is another way to show that you really want the opportunity and that you are willing to invest in yourself. I realize there are very few people that have enough money to buy plane tickets to fly across country, but this may be your first time in trying to sell someone. Try to sell your family on assisting with your interview. If you truly want a career in this business, you are going to have to work for it.

For your interview, be sure to dress the part. Make sure you take some of your hard-earned money and buy a nice suit/shirt/tie/dress/etc. You don't want to stroll into an interview wearing khaki's and a polo; that's not going to cut it. Make sure you iron your clothes, shine your shoes, do your hair, etc. Take a quick look in the mirror and make sure you are looking better than normal.

Now you have your attire set up and ready to go, next step is doing research on the company you are interviewing with. It is very easy to simply type the team name in your web browser and start taking notes. Is it necessary to know all of the players on the team? No, but you also don't want to be asked to name 2 players and not be able to do that. If you really want the job, you will need to know a little bit about the team and what they are currently doing from a business perspective. For example, take a look at their ticket sales page and see the following:

- What teams/events are playing at the specific arena/stadium?
- What types of ticket plans do they offer?
- What does their seating chart look like?
- What are the different price points they have?
- What type of premium seating do they have?
- What type of hospitality options they have?
- What type of group programs do they offer?
- What promotions do they have with their schedule?

Again, you don't need to memorize all of the above items, but it will help you to have an understanding of the role you are going into. After looking through the website of the team, do some research on the people you are interviewing with as well. Check out LinkedIn, the front office chart, etc. Don't be creepy, but it's always nice to know where they were beforehand and the different positions they have held in their careers. Majority of the time you are able to immediately find a connection that will help you initiate a conversation.

In this industry, you always want to be prepared and that should start with having a list of questions to ask at your interview. Compile a list of questions to bring with you, and be sure to type them up. You don't want the hiring manager thinking you jotted down a list of questions right before you got in that morning. Going into an interview prepared will also allow the hiring manager to see what type of person you are and what type of salesperson you will be.

Below is a list of recommended questions and a short reason what you hope to get out of them:

➤ What does an All-Star look like for this position?
   ▸ This is a great question in helping you figure out what the manager looks for and also what you want to make sure you can do on a daily basis.
➤ How do the stars that work for you differentiate themselves?
   ▸ When given the opportunity, you want to make sure you are completely ready and will once again be the star. If the hiring manager says the stars are the individuals that make the most phone calls and set the most appointments, then you want to make sure you are doing that.
➤ What are your top 3 expectations for this role?
   ▸ Again, this is a great way to figure out what is going to be expected from you and how you can make sure you meet each and every one of the expectations.
➤ What is the culture like? What are the core principles?
   ▸ What type of environment do you want to work for/ be involved in? Odds are you want to go into sales because you are competitive, so you want to make sure you are going into a competitive environment.
➤ What products are you focusing on selling more? How many appointments are the reps attending per week?
   ▸ Another great question to help you figure out what

your day to day is going to be like. The hope is that you have the ability to be a full-menu consultant with the ability to sell everything so you can put yourself in the best position for future opportunities. I will explain the value in appointments later, but in my opinion this is a #1 priority in making sure you are able to have success in meeting face to face.

➤ How am I going to be graded? What are their expectations for me?
  ▸ As you can see, most of these questions are geared towards what is expected from you on a daily basis and what you can do to stand out amongst your peers.

➤ Are there opportunities for growth in this position?
  ▸ You are choosing a team based on what type of opportunities could present themselves if you go above and beyond the call of duty and exceed expectations. It's very important to make sure there is some potential room to grow internally or at the very least get help when it comes time to look externally.

Above are questions that you should ask, but there are also several that you should *not* ask:

- What benefits do you offer?
- How much vacation time do you offer?
- Can I work from home?
- Does the company monitor internet usage?
- What is the stress level in the office?
- Do you drug test?

- Do you check references?
- Why should I take this job?

I am sure you can think of many more. Don't ask questions that don't make any sense to the job in hand. I would guess that 99% of the time, the hiring manager or the HR rep will tell you every single thing you would need to know about the potential job opportunity.

If you take anything out of this chapter, please be sure to type and prepare for the interview with questions and research that you have done. Also, make sure you have taken the time to prepare your answers for the interview, as well as to provide testimonials on topics that you may be asked for. Below is a list of some sample questions that may be asked. Be sure to go through each of these to identify and the answers that you would like to provide and practice. Remember the old saying, practice makes perfect.

Sample interview questions:

- Tell me why you chose XYZ University?
- Looking back, how was your experience, and would you choose that school again?
- Why are you interested in working in sports?
- Why are you interested in working in sales?
- Why do you think you'd be successful at sales?
- Describe your sales process to me.
- What motivates you to succeed?
- How coachable are you?
- How do you deal with rejection?
- Do you love to win or hate to lose?
- What has been your biggest accomplishment to date?

- What has been your biggest disappointment to date? How have you dealt with and overcome this?
- Give me an example of a time you have went above and beyond.
- If you don't get this job, what type of job would you look for?
- What do you hope to gain from this experience? What short/long term goals do you have?

When the big day finally arrives, above all *don't be late*. Figure out how long it will take you to arrive and look to arrive at least a half hour before. Plan on going into the office 15 minutes prior. If you get there early, you can always take some time to freshen up and do some studying. You don't want to be caught running through the doorway, dripping with sweat...Not a good first impression. Make sure you bring plenty of resumes on nice paper with spelling and grammar check completed. Have enough copies for everyone, you don't want to say I ran out of resumes, binders, etc. It's always nice to create business cards with your information on as well. This business is about differentiating yourself from the competition. Leave them with a lasting impression.

As you walk into the office, make sure you are polite and respectable. You should be the one holding the door; you should be the one saying please and thank you. Get to know the receptionist or security guard; you never know how your connections will help you along the way. Maybe the receptionist is great friends with the hiring manager, and in passing they talk to them about how nice you were, how professional you acted, and how you would be a great fit for their company.

The format of the interview can vary depending on the company. You may meet with leaders and representatives individually. You may meet a group of them. You may be with other candidates in group interviews. You may even partake in the type of interviews I always ran, where it was the day and life of a professional sports sales executive. In this type of interview, you go through scripting, role playing, and even get on the phones to make actual cold calls. Regardless of the type of interview you are going to partake in, be sure to come with you're A-game. Smile, sit up, and be engaged. Hiring managers do not want to see some slouched, with a frown on their face, and doodling on a notepad. As you meet each individual, be sure to hand them a business card and resume, give them a firm handshake, and thank them for taking the time to sit with you.

As you sit across from the interviewer, be honest with all of your answers and show excitement . You shouldn't have to read word for word off your resume; the story you are telling is what you have accomplished in your short life. TELL YOUR STORY.

Be sure to always ask questions to every person that interviews you. One of my biggest pet peeves is when I ask someone if they have any questions and they say no or that they have already had all of their questions answered. Don't think you know everything about the position; there are plenty of things for you to learn. That is exactly why you have already had a list of questions drawn out. And be sure to write down the information they are telling you; you won't remember everything they say.

"Let's be honest", "You know", "Um"….any idea why I wrote those short phrases down? Those are 3 main things you should never say in an interview. When a candidate says, "Let's be honest", first thing an interviewer thinks is that perhaps they were stretching the truth or lying with all of the other answers they gave. When a candidate says, "You know", odds are the interviewer doesn't know. That is why they are asking you the question. In a sales position, you need to confident, and "Um…" doesn't sound confident at all. Eliminate all of those words from your vocabulary.

As you interview, make sure you let each and every person know how are excited you are about the opportunity and that you truly do want the position. Don't be afraid to ask questions, and make sure you see the office in its entirety as well as the arena/ballpark/stadium. If you are going to be selling for a franchise, you want to see firsthand what you are going to have to sell. When leaving the interview, you want to make sure everything has been answered and, if offered, you could make an educated decision on your first opportunity.

As you are leaving the interview, again thank the interviewees for their time, obtain their business cards, and find out what the next steps are. In sales, you never want to walk away from an appointment without asking for the close, so why not start the sales process early and ask for the job?

"Thank you so much for your time today. I have really enjoyed getting to meet with everyone and learn more about the opportunity and what is to be expected from an All-Star. Based on our meeting today, what do you think I could improve on and ultimately do you feel that I can do the job?"

When you finally leave and the stressful day is behind

you, remember that you're not done yet. Make sure you follow up with a handwritten thank you card and an email to EVERY single person you met with. Also, be sure to follow up with the hiring manager when they asked you to. Don't be overbearing and call everyday, but make sure they know you definitely want the position.

1. Invest in your future. Dress, Transportation, Preparation.
2. Practice your interview questions and answers.
3. Ask for the job!

CHOOSING THE BEST FIT

After you make it through the interview process for one job, you may not be completely done. Hopefully you have several more lined up which multiple teams in multiple cities. Make sure you do as much preparation as you did for the first one as you will do for the last one. This should be an exciting time for you; don't stress out too much, and enjoy the journey.

As you continue interviewing, some hiring managers will likely ask you what other teams you are talking to/interview with. As always, be up front and honest with them. You should be proud of the fact that you have the ability to interview with multiple teams. To let you in on a little secret, the hiring managers certainly don't mind either. We are competitive, so we want to make sure we are hiring the best talent and if other teams are interviewing them, then we tend to believe that they are a decent candidate.

Hopefully you have the opportunity to go through several interviews and get multiple offers. The best advice

I can offer you is to go into each interview, knock it out of the park, and walk away with several offers. Then YOU can make the decision that is best for you personally and professionally, rather than just taking a job because it was the only one you were offered.

If you are fortunate enough to obtain several offers, congratulations! However, you are now going to have a tough decision to make but a very exciting one as well. I have always found it best to create a pro and con list for both your personal and professional life. At the end of the day, you ultimately need to make the best decision for you and nobody else. Below are some key points that will hopefully help you make the best decision for you both personally and professionally.

- ➤ Where is the job located?
  - ▸ Are you willing to relocate? Are you willing to move several states away from your family and friends?
    - ▷ This decision has to come from you and nobody else. I would strongly recommend be willing to relocate, as this will increase the amount of opportunities. You're young—go out and see the world! You can always come back home down the road.
    - ▷ Is it a city that you can see yourself in? Can you get involved in activities outside of the office? You are moving for the job, but you also want to make sure you can be happy in your free time. Also, a new place would be a good place for your friends and family to come visit.
- ➤ What is the job?
  - ▸ Is it something you can get up every morning and

be excited and passionate about? Don't worry about the title; figure out what your responsibilities and expectations are going to be.

➤ Who you are working for?
  ▸ In my opinion, this is one of the most important questions you need to answer. Who is your direct boss? Who else in the company is going to have an impact on your career? You want to choose to work for the right people that have your career interests in mind and can train and teach you everything you need to know so you have a long career ahead of yourself.

➤ What is the opportunity?
  ▸ Is there inventory available? You want to make sure you are going to a place that you have the ability to sell prime real estate, not just seats upstairs, and have the ability to bring in new business, not just renew accounts.

➤ Are there opportunities for career growth?
  ▸ If you go into the job, crush your goals and bring all of the intangibles to the table, will you have the opportunity to grow your career whether it is internally or externally? Remember this isn't just a job you are signing up for; it should be the first step in your long career in this industry.

As you internalize all of your personal feelings as well as other people you trust, look to make the decision based on your gut feeling. At the end of the day, my advice is to take a role that is around the right people, a great opportunity, and you have the ability to make an impact. I am a firm believer that people lead; title, responsibility, and money will follow as long as you surround yourself with the right people. I am sure you grew up following a favorite team, but don't automatically think that is going to be the best opportunity for you. That specific team might not have the right people in place, the right opportunity for you, or the best first career step for you.

Odds are you won't be working for teams that have multiple championships in the past several years. They don't need us; they are already sold out. You are probably going to work for teams that are not very good on the field. That's ok, though, because you are in sales to sell experience, not wins or losses. You are not interviewing for the starting point guard, quarterback, pitcher, or general manager; you are interviewing for a sales professional position. Think about how exciting it would be to sell out tickets for a team that isn't good and hasn't been in a long time. That shows what type of true salesperson you really are.

Once you make the decision, do not look back or have second guesses; you have done your research and made the decision that is best for you and your family. If you were the fortunate one to have several offers, make sure you tell the teams that you are declining the right way. As I mentioned earlier, you should have been up front and honest the entire time, so all of the teams should know that there are other opportunities out there for you.

Make sure you call the other teams, no email or letters. You never know when your paths may cross again so you don't want to burn a bridge. When calling them, thank them for their time and for putting you through the process. Let them know that after thinking through the different opportunities and pros and cons, you have decided to start your career with a different organization.

Again, congratulations this is an awesome time in your life. You did spend the last several years in college hoping for a job and you have done it BUT you haven't made it. It is only the beginning.

1. Put yourself in a position where you get to make the decision.
2. Focus on who you are working for, the opportunity, and career growth.
3. Be excited – your journey is beginning!

CHAPTER 3

STARTING YOUR CAREER

I graduated college on May 12th and moved to Atlanta on May 13th and had a few weeks before my June 4th start date with the Atlanta Hawks and Thrashers. First let me tell you, moving from a small farm town to a big city like Atlanta was a big adjustment in more ways than one. Regardless, I moved down to Atlanta with only some clothes, a dresser, and a TV. But it didn't matter because I had my dream job. I was working for a professional sports team!

As I was getting into the business, I knew one thing and that was I needed to be successful and make money. How to do that? Find mentors that I can gravitate towards and learn from. Be the hardest worker and outwork everyone. Invest in myself each and every day. Hustle was going to be a key to my success and that is what I focused on each and every day. I prided myself on being the first one in and last one out, I thrived on winning the hustle contest every week, and I spent time in non-working hours practicing my scripts, studying product knowledge, and reading to do everything I could to be elite and standout from day one.

In my experience in this business, I have heard people

say, "Well, I work smarter not harder." What does that mean? How all of a sudden do you become smarter? In this business, you will become more efficient and effective by working harder and gaining more exposure on how to better yourself in everyday tasks as well as areas of the business. That takes time, determination, sweat and struggle; it will in turn make you work smarter and more effective. However, I am here to tell you that if you work harder, you will become smarter, and be a lot more satisfied with your work.

In this chapter, I will show you what it's like to start out in the business. This should be able to give you insight on what you should do to prepare for every first day you have in this business.

PREPARING FOR THE FIRST DAY

Most Inside Sales positions will be a 9-12-month program and you will start out at $8-$12 an hour with no benefits and the ability to make commission on sales. This probably isn't the salary you dreamed about when you first get out of college but it's the reality if you want to start a dream job in professional sports. I am not going to try to be your parents but make sure you are smart with your money especially when you first start off as moving to a new city can be a big financial burden. Most apartments you will be required to pay first month's rent plus a deposit, so you need to have some money saved up. Odds are that you will move to a new city to start your career and you will have to buy furniture, accessories, etc. along the way.

As you begin to prepare for your first day of work, don't spend all the time in the world partying in your brand-new city. Focus on getting to know the terrain. Take some time to drive around to see the different office buildings, restaurants, events, etc. because you never know who your next potential client could be. If you are starting with a group of people, get their phone numbers and information and set up a time to meet with everyone. This business is a lot about relationships and the sooner you begin to build them, the better off you will be.

In most sports sales' programs, you are required to dress business casual/professional. The world has certainly evolved, and I know many of my colleagues will call me old school, but I always wear a suit and tie. It's always easier to dress down once you get to a meeting than try to dress up. For men, this requires a shirt and tie everyday, so make sure you have a fully stocked wardrobe. I have certainly agreed to disagree with people over the years, but I would strongly recommend being suited up for every meeting. You are young, so you need to at least look the part.

Throughout the interview process and the job acceptance, you may have received different materials or documents regarding your employment and position. Make sure you sign and turn in any documents right away. On the sales end, if you were given a script, be sure to take the several weeks leading up to your first day and do a lot of role playing. plan to go into the first meeting and role play the script like you have been doing it for years.

Another key component in ticket sales is product knowledge. You can't expect to sell something if you don't know the product, including the locations and pricing. Go on to the team's website and print off the seating charts and study them. Know the ballpark/arena/field like it's in your backyard. Also, in most Inside Sales programs, you are going to have the ability to sell season ticket plans, groups, and even suites, so start studying the pricing. The sooner you can present locations and price, the quicker you will be on the phone making sales and making money.

The best way to get good with product knowledge is like anything you do in life, study and practice. Act like the first day of you work are having an exam and if you don't pass, you have to retake your senior year over. Now I know that probably sounds great but that includes you have to pay for your senior year again. To ultimately be successful in this industry, you need to put the time and effort into it.

1. Save money to start your new life.
2. Begin to immerse yourself in the city.
3. Study and wow the organization from the start.

DAY 1

You probably think your first day in the real world will be pretty easy. You'll have some paperwork to complete, introductions, getting to know the staff, going over the syllabus, maybe even getting out early. NEWS FLASH – this is the real world, and you are there to get a job done. There is a lot to learn on the first day, and you need to be ready to go from day one.

One of the rules that I still adhere to today is to be on time, every time. With that being said, make sure you plan out your trip accordingly. Give yourself enough time if traffic is bad. If your day starts at 8:30am, plan to arrive to the office no later than 8:15am so you can get yourself prepared for the day. If you are taking the train or bus, make sure you know the exact time it leaves and what stop you need to get off. I'm sure this sounds pretty easy, but you would be surprised how difficult it is for some people to show up to work on time.

Finally, 8:30am arrives and it's time for your first day in the real world. Don't get scared now, this was the time you have been waiting on your whole life. You have started your dream job, it's now a reality, but don't stop now; you have a lot to learn and a long way to go to really make it in this industry. Just like when you were playing sports, you shouldn't walk casually to where you need to go. Be alert and ready to go. You don't need to sprint to the conference room, but make sure you are not the last one in. And absolutely don't be late.

Many guidelines to follow for the first day need to be followed throughout your career no matter what position you are in. You should always be the first one to volunteer for anything the manager asks, no matter how small of a task it may seem. Doing little things like volunteering will help you begin to make a name for yourself. There is a big difference in helping out and brown nosing/sucking up, but being proactive is never a bad thing.

Typically, managers and other members of the different sales staff will come down to welcome you to the family on your first day. There are 2 things you can do when this happens. You can try to be the class clown and make a name for yourself that way, or you can be professional from the start and answer the questions in the way they were intended to be answered. This will be your first experience in communicating with the other managers and reps, so make sure you come across as an individual that could ultimately work alongside them.

Many teams will provide you a playbook on the first day and this is not like a college syllabus, where you may never review it again. This should be something that your first several weeks you should take home on a nightly basis and really focus on getting better every single day. One of the sections of the training manual will be about expectations and this is something to take to heart. If you want to be the best, you need to go above and beyond. Below is a small sample size of some of the expectations that are going to be given to you and each and every day.

- Be on time, at your desk and making calls at the beginning of your day
- Minimum of 75 calls per day
- Minimum of 2 hours of talk time per day
- Set 10 face-to-face meetings per week
- Complete 5 face-to-face meetings per week
- Gain 10 referrals per week
- Send 25 hand-written cards per week
- Bring a consistent positive attitude and strong work ethic each day
- Effectively manage your time and be organized
- Accurately manage your pipeline
- Have a team focus – sell out the ballpark/arena/ stadium together
- Conduct yourself with class at all team functions
- Always under promise and over deliver
- Have fun!!!

Early on in this chapter, I walked about working hard and not letting anyone outwork you. Hopefully it's pretty self-explanatory but being able to work harder and smarter should be as simple as some of the following:

- Come in early, stay late
- Minimum of 100 calls per day
- Minimum of 2 and a ½ hours of talk time per day
- Set 15 face-to-face meetings per week
- Complete 8 face-to-face meetings per week
- Gain 15 referrals per week
- Send 40 hand-written cards per week
- Always have a positive attitude and strong work ethic
- Effectively manage your time and be organized
- Accurately manage your pipeline and continue to grow it
- Have a team focus – sell out the ballpark/arena/stadium together
- Conduct yourself with class at all team functions
- Always under promise and over deliver
- Have fun!!! You will have more fun when you have more success!

Remember, this is Day 1 of a hopefully long career. If you are reading this and you are already questioning the work involved, you may want to think about a different career path. For those who feel excited by the challenge, remember not to be too eager, and don't bury yourself in work too early. In order to make that first phone call, go on the first appointment, make that first sale, you need to make sure you are ready to take every step necessary and have complete confidence in your pitch. Practice makes perfect.

1. Be on time. ALWAYS.
2. Pay attention and take notes.
3. Study.

THE FIRST FEW WEEKS

The first several weeks as an entry-level salesperson are very training oriented. A lot of information will be thrown your way, so make sure you are coachable and committed to learning each and every second of the day.

Throughout the first week, your direct manager will probably tell you quite a few stories about his/her career as well as other successful people in the business. I usually call these the Day and Life of X, as everyone will walk you through the struggles and successes they have had. They are not telling you these stories to brag; they are telling you because they have been in your shoes and have found a way to thrive in the industry. Make sure you are taking notes and finding ways to replicate their strategies and ideas. As always, be prepared to ask intelligent questions.

We have talked a lot about how you should be as an individual and what YOU need to do every day to make it in this business. However, you also have to realize that you still work for a sports team, which means you have to be able to collaborate and work alongside each other to make it the most successful team. I am not asking for you to become best friends with everyone you work with; I am asking that you are a team player and can work collectively as a group to be a very successful unit.

The most successful entry-level sales reps are the ones

that take their lunch breaks early on and walk around the arena to learn everything about it. Start sitting in different sections so you can paint the picture of the view, identify where the escalators, restrooms, and different foods options are located. Once you gain a good grasp of where everything is located, and then start diving into the different price points are located and start familiarizing yourself with the cost of the seat.

As you go through the initial activities and product knowledge training, make sure you are taking detailed notes and going back through all of the items so you can become the "expert". Some people apply for specific jobs because they already know a lot about a certain team or sport, but this isn't always necessary. Whatever you don't know, you can always learn.

Many programs will have you start out by doing team building or sales activities. Make sure you are taking the time and your due diligence to really think through the process and immediately make an impact. How do you make an impact? The impact will be by leading the charge and going first, by showing that you took the time to follow ALL of the directions, and most importantly that you understand what the activity entails. Many of the activities will involve sales techniques. This is a test to see what type of sales skills you already have. One piece of advice: if you are given a glass to sell, don't immediately go into selling the benefits of the glass. Sales is all about being a consultant and asking questions. Think about what types of questions you can ask in regard to that. For example, what type of glass are you currently using? How do you like it? What do you like most about it? How often do you utilize a glass per day? There are many different questions you can ask and from there you will learn more about your prospect and then can pitch an appropriate glass with benefits. Most importantly, make sure you are having fun!

As your first few weeks continue, you will be introduced to several different scripts. I know your first thought is probably *if I just read right off of a script, I am going to sound like a robot and there is no chance I can sell*. I can tell you from experience that this isn't true. These scripts came around a long time before you and will continue to stay around a long time after you. The goal of a script is to give you a roadmap through the call, appointment, process, etc. Eventually you will be able to internalize it and make it your own.

Over the next few chapters, we will break down some of the different types of scripts and the most beneficial ways to utilize them on a consistent basis. I am going to walk through the scripts that I feel are most beneficial and that I have learned and taught from. Regardless of the team you start out with, your sales scripts may be a bit different. Again, the main goal of a script is to give you a platform to be able to walk through the details of the process and will help you always lead the call or appointment in the right direction. Much of being successful in this business is having the ability to think on your feet and be able to ad lib, but the scripts give you a firm place to start.

1. Be a team player.
2. Be a consultant.
3. Internalize the scripts and make them your own.

CHAPTER 4

THE BASICS OF SELLING

After a few years in leadership, I was given the opportunity to be the Vice President of Ticket Sales and Service for the Phoenix Suns of the NBA and Phoenix Mercury of the WNBA as well as an Arena Football League team and an NBA G-League Team. This was my first opportunity to oversee the entire ticketing landscape so it was important for me to not only continue to hustle and be efficient but also have all of the different areas of the business moving in the right direction. With myself and each team member having goals and responsibilities for multiple properties, it was important to go in with the right mindset and really understand how the flow of a successful conversation should go. Finally, sales is never going to be easy but the most successful individuals are the ones that can overcome objections and find ways to win every day!

Now that you have your dream job, it's time to learn how to succeed. In this chapter, I will share with you the secret to becoming a great salesperson and how you need to continue to find ways to be successful.

HAVING A SALES AND SERVICE STATE OF MIND

As I have already discussed, much of this business is to go in with the right mindset. At the end of the day, selling is not a very complex process; it's just difficult to do on a consistent basis.

It's very important to start with having the right mindset and mentality as you go into each day. Having that right mindset starts with being prepared prior to each outreach.

That's why whether you regard it as an art or a science, the discipline of selling starts with the setting of a pre-call objective. Make sure you have an idea of the reason you are about to make the outreach each and every time. If anyone doubts this, remember that, by definition, a sales call must move systematically toward a sale. In some cases, it only takes a few seconds before a call, but on every occasion, it's vital for the sales member to answer one simple question: "If this call is successful, what will the result be?"

Taking the time to do this starts the selling process in motion. Before every sales call, ask yourself, "What am I going in here for? What is the result I'm trying to get to happen? If they give me the opportunity, what am I going to recommend?"

How many of you went into a test in college without looking at the notes? Ok, maybe don't answer that, but be real with yourself. How much easier would it have been had you taken a few minutes to prepare?

Focus and Flexibility:

Writing down your pre-call objective increases the focus of your efforts. Given today's evolving marketplace, this focus is essential. If salespeople are just going around visiting

48

customers to see what develops, they are merely well-paid tourists. If they are professional sales representatives, they should be moving the customer in the direction of a pre-determined goal.

Knowing where you are going definitely increases the likelihood of getting there. Obviously, if the pre-call objective turns out to be inappropriate as the sales call develops, it's easy to switch tactics. Often such a change involves simple redirection.

Make the goal specific:

When asked the purpose of a call, some salespeople will say enthusiastically, "It's to get a sale. Let's go!" Of course, everyone's in favor of getting sales, but that's more likely to happen if salespeople stop and ask themselves, "What is the need of this prospect I can try and serve? Which product or service is best for this account? How large an order should I go for? The more specific the objective, the better.

Many salespeople have told me they will only take the time to really plan out prior to an in-person meeting. I find this shortsighted. After all, if you don't go into the call prepared, you will never get the chance to have a meeting.

Set an objective for every call:

Sometimes the sales call has a limited objective. Guiding the customer in the direction of the pre-planned outcome is what I see experienced salespeople doing on most sales calls. They do it with such simple questions as: "I will be in your area next Tuesday, how about I swing by and learn more about your business and see if there is a mutual fit?"

It's amazing how often even veteran salespeople skip the pre-call objective step in favor of just seizing whatever opportunities seem to present themselves. As a professional, it's your responsibility to head off this kind of behavior. Commit to having an objective for every call, and after a call check your results against the objective.

This is a simple truth that the best sales professionals have known all along. The most important step in a sale takes place without the customer ever being there. A pre-call objective can be as simple as taking a quick glance at LinkedIn to see where they work, what school they went to, and what hobbies they are interested in. The next step is identifying what type of face-to-face opportunity you are going to look to present. All of that should be done under 2 minutes. Now that you have done a bit of prep work – go at it!

1. Have the right mindset to win your day.
2. Be focused at all times.
3. Have a pre-call objective every time.

Individual Buyer Script

As you begin your career, most teams will start you off by teaching you how to work with individual buyers. These are buyers that have been to games in the past and they have purchased tickets online, through secondary marketplaces, etc. and the sales representative will now follow up with them to learn about their experience. The main objective of a phone call is to build a relationship with the potential customer and find the best ticket fit for them.

Below is an example of an individual buyer script.

"Hi <CUSTOMER'S NAME> this is _____ with the front offices of <XXX> Arena and the <TEAM NAME>. (PAUSE) Great to speak with you today, because <CUSTOMER'S NAME> I am calling as your personal consultant for this season! I wanted to reach out and personally thank you for your support, and I'd love to find out a little more about your memories with us. I'm curious, <CUSTOMER'S NAME>, what's your favorite memory at an <XXX> game?"

As you start the dialogue with the prospect and engage in the relationship building stage, additional open-ended questions include:

- "How and when did you fall in love with 'the sport'"?
- "Who do you come to games with?"
- "How many people do you normally comes to games with?"
- "If I gave you the keys to <ARENA/BALLPARK/ STADIUM>, where would you sit?"
- "Who is your favorite player and why?"
- "How many games would you ideally like to attend per month?"
- "Which days of the week work best for you? Weekends or weekdays?"
- "What do you do for a living?"
- "What do you like to do for fun in the city?"
- "What do you enjoy most about coming to games?"

Once you have established a rapport with the customer, clearly define the benefits you are offering with a short statement:

"Great <u><CUSTOMER'S NAME></u>, what I do is I specialize in working with individuals like yourself and find out what they liked/ disliked: really help to customize programs using our member benefits to best fit them. We have a great membership model that provides year-round benefits to our members and greater flexibility during the season with our game exchange program and online account manager... <u><CUSTOMER'S NAME>,</u> I would love to host you on a VIP tour of <ARENA/BALLPARK/STADIUM>. After the tour, we'll sit down and discuss all of our new options for this upcoming season."

"<u><CUSTOMER'S NAME>,</u> looking at my schedule I have <DATE & TIME> and<DATE & TIME>. Which works best for you?"

I know what you're thinking: *I am going to sound like a robot if I read that same script over and over again!* Think about it from the other side, though; odds are that the customer on the phone has probably never had a customer service type of call like this, so they have no idea what you are saying the same thing every time. The only person that knows is you and the people around you that are having similar calls.

I am going to say this now and I will probably repeat it over and over: this script, in addition to the other scripts, will work. It's proven. It has been used in this business before I got here, and it will certainly still be used long after I am gone. Each team will have a similar script. Some of the language may be different, but the main focus is to get to know the customer, build a relationship, and find a way to get face to face.

Now, let's go over the script and explain the what/why/how behind each statement and question. First, go back and reread the script and try putting yourself on the other end. If you were the customer, think about why some of the questions/statements are important.

"I am calling as your personal consultant for the season..."

The first sentence is the most vital in the entire phone call. When you are calling an individual buyer or anyone for that matter, you have 10 seconds to get their attention. Think about it: how many times are you caught off guard with a phone call? When you are first calling someone, you need to come with energy, enthusiasm, and be quick, precise, and to the point.

In the first sentence, it's quick and easy. Here is who I am what, what I do, and why I am calling. The entire phone call process is a game of hot potato, you want to quickly say what you need to say and then put the ball back in their court to use a sports analogy. Chris Zaber (a wise man) once told me that you have two ears and one mouth for a reason; you should do twice as much listening as you do talking. This should hold true for every phone call that you are on.

"What is your favorite memory?"

Why do you think this is the first question to ask? The main reason is it will be very hard for someone to answer that negatively. Each and every call you want to think of being on a staircase. How do you get to the top of a staircase?

You keep climbing up, and once you get to the top you have set the meeting. So, start by asking positive thought questions where you can continue to climb upwards.

Think about if you would start with a question "Do you want to come out to more games?" That could open a can of worms where they start bashing the team, their experience, etc. and now it's going to be much more difficult to get to the top of the steps.

Before diving into the additional questions, I also want to hit on another question I always get which is why don't we ask, "Is this a good time?" or "How are you doing?". I realize this is how you were taught or that is the way you always talk to people when you reach out to them but let's go back to there is 10 seconds to make an impact. At the end of the day, you probably have never met or spoken with this person, so do you really care how they are doing? Do they feel comfortable actually telling you? Remember, at the end of the day, we are in sales and people on the other line are going to know you're a sales individual. Don't give them an easy out by asking if they have time. Also, think about the different ways a simple "How are you doing?" could go. It could be an easy answer of good, fine, ok, not good. Where do you go from there? Or it can be dramatic, "Not good, my wife left me, my dog ran away, and my kid can't find his shoes." Again, where do you go from here?

The main point is to stick to the script – identify yourself, why you are calling, and dive into finding out about their best memory. With any of the questions we are going to discuss, be sure to put yourself in their shoes and think about the answers not only that you would provide but also how the answers would help you stay on the staircase.

"How and when did you fall in love with <SPORT>?

Now to the sport question, think about how you would answer? More times than not, the answer is probably about growing up watching/playing with your family/friends/etc. Similar to the best memory, this question will probably lead to positive answers, which continues to help build the relationship. This question will also get you insight into them as an individual.

"Who do you come to games with?"

Many times, some of the questions will already be answered based on the best memory and sport question. However, by asking who you go to games with; this will help get to know the customer better as many times they will discuss going with their friends, family, kids, etc. Plus, it gives you a great opportunity to start identifying and understanding how many seats they may need.

"How many people do you normally comes to games with?"

Similar to the question before, this is going to help you identify how many seats for what a package may look like. You may think, well why do I ask both when they could be similar answers. You would be surprised as many times you ask both of these questions and you will get two different answers. The more you can get the customer to talk about different experiences and different people, the more it will help you in the long term if the objection starts to become there are too many games/too many seats; you will have other leverage to discuss about how they can utilize. We will get to objections later but think about how each of the questions can become long-term partnership opportunities.

"If I gave you keys to the <ARENA/BALLPARK/STA-DIUM>; where would you sit?"

This is one of the most basic questions that you can ask and as you can imagine, you should really be able to see how someone's personalities work. I like asking this in the middle because typically this question helps continue to break down the barriers. You may hear courtside, right behind home plate, 50-yard line, etc. They also may say, "but I know I can't afford it" and BOOM—this is the start of the buying process. Being on the team side, with membership packages you are able to get well-valued seats at less than what they typically pay. In general, this question starts getting them to continue to imagine their experience at your venue.

"How many games would you ideally like to attend per month?"

This is one of my favorite questions because this really helps the potential customer understand the value and commitment to join your family. Many people will automatically think 3-4 games per month. On a baseball end, that equates to a 20-game plan. For basketball or hockey, that would be a 13-game plan or half-season. For football, that's pretty much a full-season. Now this is typically when customers talk about their lowest point of entry, so this number can always rise as you get into the buying process.

"Which days of the week work best for you? Weekends or weekdays?"

As you can see, most of the questions are very self-explanatory. Even so, I hope you can see the value of each of the questions. As I discussed earlier, product knowledge is very important, and most teams will have a plan that focuses on weekdays/weekends. Plus, with this question (if it hasn't come out earlier) you will also learn more about their family/friends and additional activities that will be vitally important for referrals (more on that later).

"What do you do for a living?"

If you haven't already found out, get to know the customer more and what they and their families do for a living. This will also be crucial in understanding the business landscape because this individual buyer may quickly turn into a business or group buyer as well.

"What do you and your family/friends enjoy most about coming to games?"

I like to call this the t-ball question as you might as well put the ball on the tee and crush it out of the ballpark when it comes to this. We already discussed how starting with a best memory puts the conversation on a positive track. Now, you are almost to the top of the stairs so let's lay another easy positive momentum question. This is a crucial question to make sure you write down the answer because this will assist in the closing process. Be sure to find out not only what the customer likes but also what everyone else enjoys most when they attend as there are going to be more than one person involved in the buying process.

You are nearing the top of the staircase now lay down the hammer with the benefit statement. It basically reiterates your intro line with why you called them, asked them questions, and are now ready to get face-to-face and show them the value of being a part of the family.

Saying the benefit statement is equally as important as

saying the introduction lines. Have passion and energy and show excitement. Remember, you are still on the phone and you probably aren't seeing them via video so you need to ensure your voice comes across just as excited as they should be. I want you to do a quick project. In a low, non-energetic tone; read the benefit statement:

> "Great <u><NAME></u>, what I do is I specialize in working with individuals like yourself and find out what they liked/ disliked: really help to customize programs using our member benefits to best fit them. We have a great membership model that provides year-round benefits to our members and greater flexibility during the season with our game exchange program and online account manager... <u><NAME></u>, I would love to host you on a VIP tour of <ARENA/BALLPARK/ STADIUM>. After the tour, we'll sit down and discuss all of our new options for this upcoming season."

> <u>"<NAME></u>, looking at my schedule I have <DATE & TIME> and <DATE & TIME>. Which works best for you?"

What do you think? Would you agree to a meeting after that? Sounds like the worst first date ever.

Now reread the benefit statement with passion and energy.

"Great <u><NAME></u>, what I do is I specialize in working with individuals like yourself and find out what they liked/ disliked: really help to customize programs using our member benefits to best fit them. We have a great membership model that provides year-round benefits to our members and greater flexibility during the season with our game exchange program and online account manager… <u><NAME>,</u> I would love to host you on a VIP tour of <ARENA/BALLPARK/STADIUM>. After the tour, we'll sit down and discuss all of our new options for this upcoming season."

"<u><NAME>,</u> looking at my schedule I have <DATE & TIME> and <DATE & TIME>. Which works best for you?"

How different did that sound? How much more engaging was it? How much more excited are you to meet with the customer? Plus, you probably just spent 10+ minutes on the phone building up to this point. It's time to jump on the platform and get a meeting commitment.

Finally, the commitment stage. You have now presented the VIP tour, now give them two options that work for you. This is very important. My advice is to look at your schedule prior to starting calls and pick two times that will work. Remember, you are going to book a lot of appointments so be sure to break your day up in an efficient way.

Nailed it, now you have assessed the customer, built a relationship, and set a definitive next step. Before moving on, go back and read the script in front of your mirror and make sure you have passion and energy the entire time!

1. Game of hot potato; let the customer do the talking.

2. Build relationships.
3. Get excited about the potential of a meeting.

OBJECTIONS

Why is being in the sales industry difficult? It's difficult because there are a lot of reasons people won't buy. Businesses hire sales people because they need the help selling the product.

One of the biggest reasons there are opportunities for people like you to get into the sports business is because we are selling something that is not really needed in life. Believe me, if you are anything like me, I am not sure how I would have grown up or continue to live without sports in my life, but it certainly isn't a necessity. People love to buy but hate to be sold; that's why we need to be sales consultants that can help the customer identify what they ultimately want to purchase. If you think you are going to be successful by just continuing to call until you find someone that wants to buy, you will have issues. People will buy because they like and trust you. You will need to learn to overcome objections without losing that trust.

Take a minute to think about some of the objections you may hear from a potential customer.

Did you take a minute? Maybe take one more...

Being in this business for over 12 years, I have heard objections that I don't even think I could make up. Regardless, you need to be prepared to listen to objections and then find ways to get customers to think about it from a different lens. Notice that I didn't say battle objections or fight through them. Why? Well, I can tell you one thing: I have never won a battle with a customer. They clearly have those feelings/ opinions for a reason, and it's going to be very difficult to get them to change their course. However, it's much easier for them to understand the value of the product more or think about things a little differently. Plus, why would you want to battle or fight with a future customer/friend of yours?

As you are looking to overcome objections, think about your end goal. The first end goal is to get face to face because as you can imagine it's much easier to have someone look at a different perspective when they are in the venue and their emotions are starting to help make decisions. When you are in person and now overcoming objections, the goal is to get the customer to join the family. There are four ways that I train and continue to overcome objections and that is by simply addressing the prospects concern and it's always important to address with a "Thank You":

1. "Thank you for sharing, a lot of my best customers have said the same thing."
2. "Thank you, that's good for me to know."
3. "Thank you for sharing, I can appreciate that."
4. "Thank you, I am really glad you brought that up."

No matter what type of objection the customer comes up with, you should always start with one of the four statements above. This shows that you have listened, and you are acknowledging what they have said or what their concerns are which is most important. Plus, it gives you the ability to then transition into testimonials or some ideas on how to get the prospect to think differently. However, the biggest advantage you will have in overcoming objections is making sure you listen and truly understand what they are objecting to.

As you get to the point of asking for a meeting, many times the customer may say "I don't have the time". It is very crucial to then ask the simple question of "tell me more". It's vitally important to understand if they are objecting to a particular appointment time or if they are saying they don't have time to commit to a package or plan. I have seen many sales members start handling the time objection with telling the customer some of the benefits of a package when all they really should be doing is providing additional times that they can meet face to face. Don't over analyze – think about what the objection truly is.

The other big no-no when trying to overcome an objection is starting to debate/argue about different conversation topics such as team performance or individual players. People buy sports tickets because of emotion. Why get in the habit of trying to change how they feel?. Whenever a customer starts complaining about the team or a player, that means they are passionate about it. Think about it: why would someone want to argue or debate something if they really had zero interest? Let them explain their frustrations or concerns – that shows they are paying attention to what is going on. Feel free to give your opinion on the topic, but don't be bullish with this. Having an educated dialogue is not a bad thing, but don't get into argument mode. You won't win, I promise!

When you join the team, you will spend a lot of time going over objections. I am going to share some of the common objections and some of the easy rebuttals to make but be sure to continue to practice how to overcome objections.

Objections will come and the successful salespeople know how to overcome them, get the conversation back on track, and really start climbing the steps.

Below are some of the most common objections I've heard over the years, along with responses that keep the conversation moving forward.

"I'm not interested."
"Tell me more. What is it exactly that you are not interested in?"

"That day and time doesn't work for me."
"I understand, what day works best for you?"

"I've been there before; I don't need a tour."
"How about your family or your children, how would they like to come sit in the dugout/locker-room?"

"Let me get back to you."
"That's no problem, but these VIP tours are extremely popular, and we only have specific time slots available. How about we pencil you in at <XX> time on <XX> date?"

"Are you going to try and sell me something when I'm there?"
"You are under no obligation to buy anything when you come down, no strings attached. I just want to thank you for your business, show you a side of the venue that most people don't get to see, and show you one or two different seating locations and see if there is a potential fit – what do you think?"

"We trade everyone or too many bad trades."

"I'm really glad you brought that up. The top priority for our organization is building a steady pipeline of talent that will generate sustained success in the years to come. <PROVIDE AN ADDITIONAL TALKING POINT ABOUT THE TEAMS DIRECTION> So, what do you say?"

"The team isn't any good."

"Thanks for sharing that. If I were in your position, and I thought that way, I would want to see some changes made too. When things don't go the way you want them to, you make changes… and that's exactly what we are doing. Our front office isn't afraid to make some bold moves to get the talent we need to win long-term. How cool it would be tell to say to your friends I was there when?"

"I'm not a <SPORT> fan."

"That's good for me to know. What sport are you a fan of? Which ones do you like best? Have you ever been to a live game before?"

"I can't give my tickets away."

"We can actually help with that. Many of our season ticket holders have had a lot of success using StubHub and as a season ticket holder, you will get a personal customer service rep to help you 'give your tickets away.' Plus, you will get all of the great benefits of being a season ticket holder. How great is that?"

"It's too expensive."

"I'm glad you brought that up. Is there a budget we need to stick with? We have several different options and many different price points that we can explore to find the perfect fit for you. So how does that VIP tour sound?"

"No money in the budget right now."

<PROBE MORE> "How did you allocate your entertainment dollar for this year? What types of company events do you normally do? How many deals would you need to close to make your money back on these seats?"

"I just had to lay off all of my employees."

"This IS a bad economy, but if you've noticed, the companies that aren't invested in customer service are the ones who are really struggling right now...you don't that to be you do you?"

"I've spent my entertainment budget for this year already."

<PROBE MORE> "What did you spend your entertainment budget on? How many customers do you have? What do you do to entertain your best customers?"

"I can get tickets whenever I want from the ticket window or friends."

"Sure, lots of people do that. We LOVE that you want to be here, but are you aware of all of the things you're missing out on not being a season ticket holder member?"

"I want better seats."

"I'm happy to help you. Where would you like to sit? Based on what you've told me about your budget and your location preference, here is what I recommend…."

"Traffic makes it too difficult to get there."

"I've had quite a few customers think that initially and then when they became season ticket members they were amazed at how easy it actually was. Where are you coming from each day?"

"There are too many games."

"Many of our season ticket members have taken advantage of StubHub and your personal customer service representative will help make it easier than ever for you to sell your tickets when you are not using them. It really is amazing, what do you think?"

"I buy other sports tickets and that is enough."

<PROBE MORE> "How do you use those tickets? What if I could save you money and also increase your return on investment?"

"Send me a brochure."

"Actually, the best brochures are what we have at our stadium. How about I show you everything you could need right here at the ballpark/arena/stadium?"

"I can't plan that far in advance."

"That's good for me to know. Problem is, the seats I can get you today may not be available tomorrow. The longer you wait, the less attractive seat locations become. You'll be guaranteed the very best seats NOW vs. waiting and missing out on what you really want. How about we lock in that appointment now?"

"Let me think it over."

"I can appreciate that. Let me ask you....on a scale of 1 to 10, with 10 being a "yes" today, where would you say you are on the scale? What will it take to get you to a 10?"

Why did I end with a number question? This is a question I always ask every single time. This is a question that has helped me uncover additional items or benefits that I may have missed or just something I haven't covered. No matter what number they say, it's easy to counter with another question such as "What additional information do I need to provide to get you to a 10?" or "Clearly I haven't done a good enough job explaining our overall benefit platform, what additional information provide?" The response from the customer might be "Well, I am an 8 but I need to check with my spouse." Your response, "Perfect, I am glad you see the value. Why don't we give your spouse a call right now?" or "What additional questions do you think your spouse may have that I can help answer?". This is a good opportunity to setup a follow up call/appointment with everyone on it. Or finally, why not just say, "How many times has your wife come home with purse or clothes and you won't get to enjoy those. Think about how excited she would be to have XX amount of date nights with you?" Go big or go home.

Objections will happen in 99% of your conversations or meetings. Don't worry about overcoming the objection; address it, hit on a key point, and move on. You should have noticed that every time you address an objection, you end with an open-ended question that puts the conversation back in the prospect hands. Sales will come to the people that learn how to build trust into the relationship and finalize the deal, regardless of objections.

1. Objections happen, don't get discouraged.
2. Address the concern and thank them. After all, they are spending time with you.
3. What can you do to get them to a 10?

CHAPTER 5

BUILDING RELATIONSHIPS

After starting in Atlanta and then moving to Pittsburgh, I spent my first six years in the business with people I knew very well. I then took a chance and worked for the Orlando Magic, where I didn't have connections going in. My time with the Magic really helped me understand the value of relationships. The DeVos family and leadership really focused on personal and professional balance which I was quickly able to transition into how you sell as well. In this business, you always need to take a step further to build a connection, be innovative and think outside the box, and find unique ways to meet face to face. Very few times in this business are phones just going to ring and you can make a sale. At the end of the day, we are a relationship-based business.

It's very hard to get a customer to care about you and many times it will happen over time but customers always expect you to care about them. They are going to expect you to be prepared when you meet them. Taking notes during your meeting demonstrates right away that you do indeed care about them and what they are saying. Like anything be prepared, so bring pen and paper, and be enthusiastic on learning more about them and their business and the value proposition you are willing to provide. Think about when you go out to a restaurant and someone takes your order but doesn't write it down. That doesn't impress me, it actually gives me more anxiety that something may end up getting messed up in my order. Take the time to write down the answers because, again, you are a consultant and you need to show that you are listening to all of their needs and wants to ultimately partner on the best fit.

Now that you have learned how to find prospective customers, you are ready to take this relationship to the next level. Connecting with customers is the most crucial part of our business, and in this chapter I'll show you how to do it.

I/My Statement

*"Talk to someone about themselves
and they'll listen for hours."*

This great quote from Dale Carnegie should be engrained into your memory for every time you talk with a customer.

The first step of building a relationship is getting to know someone. Many sales professionals don't realize that besides learning about the customer, it's also very important for the customer to get to know you as well. Before we get to face-to-face meetings, let's discuss I/My Statements, which are very important for you to focus on during each and every interaction with a customer. It will give them a glimpse into your life and allow both you and the customer to break down walls.

I/My Statements provide the sales member the ability to attempt to connect with the customer by offering similarities from their own life. The big thing to remember with I/My Statements is that the conversation should still be about the customer. I have seen many sales members that dive into an I/My Statement, but they don't keep it short and precise and they lose the conversation and, ultimately, the sale. These statements should be quick and to the point and then you are moving on to getting the customer to talk about themselves more.

For simplicity, I am going to share three easy I/My examples that I always utilized with the individual buyer script. It helped me to really build these out and have them be a part of my dialogue with every customer. The three easy ones can come after the following questions:

- "What's your best memory?"
- "Who do you come to games with?"
- "If I gave you keys the "arena/ballpark/stadium"; where would you sit?"

My I/My Statements for the three questions are as follows:

- "What's your best memory?"

"My favorite memory is going to watch Cal Ripken, Jr. play at Old Tiger Stadium, I was able to get his autograph, and from that day on, he was my favorite player. I always wore #8 after that."

As you can see, this is very quick and to the point. Many times, this opens up other dialogue to get to each other better because the customer may talk about their favorite player or the number they wore and why.

As soon as you finished the sentence with favorite player, go right into the next question. "How and when did you fall in love with the sport?" This is a great segue to get the customer to answer the next question or they may make a comment about your previous I/My. Regardless, the ball is back in their court and they are carrying the conversation.

- "Who do you come to games with?"

"I used to always go to games with my dad, mom, and sister. It was always a great family bonding experience, and the variety of things that go on during a sporting event helped bring us together closer."

Again, right to the point but also talks about my experience and gives the customer a glimpse into me and that I am a real human being, not just a salesperson. Lead right into the next question, but this I/My also helps you get to know the customer more because many times they will go into detail of who they are going to games with and what their family consists of. Remember: always listen!

- "If I gave you the keys to <ARENA/BALLPARK/STADIUM>; where would you sit?"

"My favorite spot to watch a basketball game is from the baseline. Growing up and playing the guard position, I always like to see the action as it goes away or is coming towards me."

Keep in mind, this is your opinion. You don't always have to agree with the customer. This shows that you are real, and you aren't just a yes man or woman. Be honest and up front about everything and that includes where you like to sit. Worst-case scenario, it may provide an opportunity for a customer to look at other options.

Again, you can in theory have an I/My for every single question that you ask. My general rule of thumb is to use only 3 I/My Statements per conversation. If you use more, you are now talking way more than you should be, and the customer has probably stopped listening. Focus on 3 that you are passionate about and really look to plug those into each and every conversation.

1. Show them you are human.
2. Prepare your I/MY Statements.
3. Use 3 per conversation.

THE POWER OF AN APPOINTMENT

As you have probably seen your entire life, when you are face to face with someone, it's just easier. I am sure I am getting some head nods right now because of the evolution of social media, dating sites, and working from home. However, think back to an example in your life when getting face to face was just much easier. Was it asking someone to prom? How about when you had a question on your homework and had to meet with the teacher after class? Learning plays in sports? Confronting a younger sibling for stealing your toys? You name it, my guess is 9 out of 10 times it will be easier to have the conversation face to face. This is no different in the sports sales business. When you get face to face with a customer, you will make more sales. More sales means more money and more success.

Earlier in the book, we discussed expectations for successful salespeople, and one of those was setting a minimum of 10 appointments per week and completing 5 of them. This is how you are going to hit your sales goals. If you want to be elite, you should be setting 15+ appointments and completing 8+. It's possible – trust me, I have seen it done.

We already discussed battling objections and finding an opportunity to still get the customer to agree to a meeting. Another big thing to focus on is ensuring you have built a thorough relationship throughout the phone conversation so when they do agree to a meeting; it's also in the individual to commit and show up to the meeting as well. Few easy steps I have taken to ensure that appointment shows up are as follows:

1. Send Calendar Invite and have the reminder set to pop up a day prior
   a. Send after 5pm
   b. *Subject Line:* Their Name/Your Name – Team **OR** Company Name/Team Meeting
      i. *Parking instructions*
      ii. *"Call me when you park so I can be in the lobby to greet you when you enter"*
      iii. *"My cell phone number is (insert cell number)"*
      iv. *"Enter the venue through XXX entrance to check in with our security desk"*

2. Send Handwritten Card
   a. Send same day of appointment booked ONLY if appointment is more than 3 days later
   b. Thank them for their time
   c. Reference something memorable from the conversation

   d. Looking forward to meeting them on (date/time)

      i. *"<PROSPECT NAME>, Thanks again for taking the time to connect on the phone today. I really enjoyed learning about <insert something you spoke about on the phone>. I'm looking forward to meeting you here at the venue on <insert date and time of appointment> and share with you all of the excitement around our organization right now. If you have any questions in the meantime please don't hesitate to let me know. All the best, <YOUR NAME>"*

3. Record a video Hype Call

   a. A hype call is not a confirmation call but a call that is going to get someone excited about meeting with you and you start painting the picture right away. If you just call to confirm the meeting, it's easy for the customer to come up with an excuse.

   b. Morning Meeting – send the afternoon before between 1-3pm

   c. Afternoon Meeting – send the afternoon before between 4-6pm

      i. *"Hey <PROSPECT NAME>, this <YOUR NAME>, your personal consultant with the team. I'm looking forward to our <time> meeting tomorrow and excited to learn more about you and your role with <COMPANY>. Our goal is to see how we can work together* *next season and share all the exciting news around our franchise that could help you achieve your goals and objectives. Ultimately, we'd love for you to join our family as we continually make positive changes to enhance our fan experiences. <PROSPECT NAME>, really appreciate you taking the time to schedule our meeting and I'll see you soon!"*

4. If they reschedule…
   a. Update the calendar invite
   b. Resend a handwritten note
      i. *Acknowledging things come up and excited to finally meet them*

Like a lot of things in this business, this may seem like a lot. But I promise you it's not. This works—just get out of your comfort zone and put the effort towards it. As you are getting ready for the big day where you will either host the potential customer or head out to their office, the preparation is vitally important. Again, do enough research to handle an intellectual conversation but don't do too much research to be creepy. Be sure to do your research on the individuals that you are meeting with, the company itself, and any recent articles that have come out. Building an agenda is crucial and shows that you care about your customer and you have taken the time to prepare. Hopefully, you are having multiple meetings per day so you will need to fill out the agenda to ensure accuracy for each and every customer meeting you have.

I try to follow the sandwich approach as a goal for each and every meeting. A sandwich is 3 parts (Personal/Business/Personal). As you will see, the agenda below starts with personal information about the individual(s) you are meeting with. Throughout this you may find out they have children, involved in leagues, etc. You then get into the objective of the meeting, which I would recommend saying every time so you understand what they want to make sure they hit on. It then hits on high level parts of the business and then the rest is to get the prospect to talk about themselves and their business. It's also very important to write down the questions you have so when you leave the meeting; you didn't forget to address anything that was important. Finally, you are ending the business part of the meeting with asking for the close and setting definitive next steps. Once you get all of it buttoned up, close it out by going back to a personal conversation that could be as easy as asking when their next game is for their child's youth sport going to be. It's always easier to walk out of the meeting with a little more of a relationship than just business. Below is a sample agenda to put together prior to every meeting.

SALES APPOINTMENT (COMPANY)
COMPANY ADDRESS

- **Name / Title:**
- **Decision Makers:**
- **Industry:**
- **Size of Company:**
- **Recent News / Approximate Yearly Rev.:**
- **Other Info:**

Objective of Meeting: Learn more about individual and company, strengths/opportunities, talk a little bit about XYZ Arena/Ballpark/Stadium, and ultimately see if there is a potential fit. Anything else you would like to add?

Likeability:

- **Where from:**
- **College:**
- **Other relatable Info:**

Creditability: (Objective Questions: goals, challenges, value of clients / make up of client base)

What Companies have inventory with us that are similar?

- Tell me a little bit more about your business? What has worked to get new business & also reward employees?
- What challenges do you foresee in the coming year?
- How many sales people do you have?
- How important is maintaining your relationships?
- What type of entertainment have you done in the past?

  ► **If YES to sports/dinner/golf/entertainment.....**
    ▷ How successful has it been? How do you utilize tickets? How many seats? What has made them successful?
    ▷ How often do you entertain on a monthly basis?
    ▷ Who usually does the entertaining for you?
    ▷ How often do you do dinners/golf? Where do you generally go?
    ▷ What has made these successful?

▷ What other ways are you currently entertaining your top clients?

Comments
- Face time is exactly what we have here
- Not trying to replace, we are trying to compliment
- Buyer Beware
- You owe it to yourself
- It would give you another outlet

Keys
- Help Grow the Business
- Increase Customer Loyalty
- Reduce Costs
- Improve Productivity
- Gain a competitive advantage

Pitch in Mind (based off any convos if applicable)**:**
Put best suite/theatre box/seating locations.
Always pitch something even if it is a thought provoking idea.

Definitive Next Step.
Put available times you have. Ask customer to get their calendar out.

When you join a team, your leaders and top successful sales Account Executives will take you on several appointments ranging from mock tours to going on live appointments riding shotgun. This is extremely beneficial as you want to take what all of the successful sales professionals are doing and mold it into your own.

As you are going through the tour, make sure you hit on key places and key talking points. Be sure to take the customer through all of the premium areas of the venue. I have heard people say, "Well, this customer didn't have the money" or "He/She was really only interested in sitting upstairs." It doesn't matter – every single prospect should be going through the same appointment process. Individual buyers may not have the budget for it, but when they see the court-side club or a luxury suite, but they might know someone who is interested or recommend it to their company. Many sales professionals have great testimonials on how they took one person on an appointment and then that individual's company ended up buying much more premium inventory.

If you have the ability to show the locker room/clubhouse or the practice court/batting cages, those are always really cool to see and the average fan typically never gets to see them. It's all about showcasing the VIP experience, because you are going to go above and beyond for your customer right from the get-go. My favorite part of a tour is taking someone down to the bench or dugout because again, not everyone can say they do that. Be sure to take some pictures; take one with your own phone, as that is a great follow-up thank you to send. The best part about taking people to those areas is you can then ask the easy questions, "Where do you like to sit in this venue? Where do you want your season tickets to be at?".

The power of face-to-face – even in today's society with so much online shopping/spending that goes on—is the in-person experience. How many big items would you buy without seeing them first-hand? Would you buy a TV without seeing the picture quality? Probably not, at the very least you are going to go to the store first to take a look before buying online. Would you ever buy a car without test-driving it? Of course not. Same holds true with a lot of customers; they probably aren't going to buy something without taking a look and actually sitting in the seats. Plus, how cool is it that the customer can literally hand pick seats out of an empty venue?

As you get into the appointment, much of the time you will reiterate some of the answers you have already received from the initial phone call. You will also want to have the prospect elaborate more and an easy way to do that is by asking the simple question of "Tell me more!". This can be asked with any question – again this is important as we are selling emotions so get them inside of the venue talking more about their best memory, their experience with their friends/family, and what they enjoy most about coming to a live sporting event. When we get into meeting with businesses later on in the book, there will be additional questions to dive into on the appointment end. For individuals, continue to learn more about their experiences, stay on the upward trajectory of the stairs, and find the best fit to join your family.

Another great way to earn more money is by cross-selling. Cross-selling can be very successful, but sales professionals get nervous that they don't want to ask for more if they have already made a sale. It is vitally important to think outside of the box, however, and view cross-selling as bonus for the customer. Many teams will offer exclusive discounts if you are already a season ticket holder/member, so you are doing yourself and the customer a disservice if you don't tell them about all of the great benefits.

Here's an example of a script you can follow: "<NAME>, it's great to have you a part of the team's family! I am looking forward to seeing you and your family at games this upcoming season. Another great benefit that comes along with your membership is the ability to get exclusive discounts on group tickets. You mentioned that you are a part of an adult basketball league. How cool would it be to get your entire league out for a game?"

Cross-selling is totally natural. Think about it: if you are happy with buying a TV at BestBuy; when it comes to buying a computer, your first choice to look will probably be BestBuy because the comfort level is there, and you trust the product. This is very similar in our business. Be the new friend or the inside source to all ticketing needs at the venue. People will buy because they like you and they see the value.

1. Getting face to face will earn more dollars.
2. Be diligent in your confirmation process.
3. Cross-Selling!

ALWAYS ASK OPEN ENDED QUESTIONS

As you can see throughout the scripts we've looked at, all questions posed to the customer are open-ended. It's easy to get lazy in this business and start asking closed ended questions, which completely kills the opportunity to walk up the steps toward a sale. Eventually you will get to the point in this business where you will even correct family members over the phone if they ask a you close-ended question.

The easiest way to think about always asking open ended questions is to focus on the 5 W's and the 1 H – Who, What, When, Where, Why, How? Below is a breakdown of a variety of different open-ended questions that you can ask in a conversation and even on an appointment. My biggest piece of advice is as you are starting out really focus on the 8-10 that you can really internalize and make your own. Then try to integrate I/My Statements, as well as anticipating objections.

Rapport Building:
- "What brought you to the city?"
- "Where do you live here in the city?"
- "What do you do professionally?"
- "What do you like to do outside of work?"
- "What's your favorite thing about living in this city?"

Family:
- "How have your kids enjoyed the giveaways?"
- "How often do you and your family get together for games?"
- "What's your kids' favorite part about coming to games?"
- "What do you know about our weekend plans to maximize time with your family?"
- "What's important to you and your family when you attend games at the venue?"
- Employees:
- "What have you done in the past to incentivize your employees?"
- "How often do you reward your employees with tickets to a sporting event?"
- "What are your thoughts about hosting a company outing here at the venue?"
- "When's the last time you took your team/department to a sporting event?"
- "What kind of experience would be important to your

employees when you attend a game?"

Prospects:
- "What industries are you currently targeting as your top prospects?"
- "How have you entertained your top prospects in the past?"
- "How often are you entertaining prospects a week/ month/year?"
- "What experience do your prospects enjoy when being entertained by you?"
- "How many sales team members do you have and what are their prospect pipeline requirements?"

Clients:
- "How have you shown appreciation to your top clients in the past?"
- "What do you to retain their business?"
- "What are you doing differently than your competitors to gain and retain your clients?"
- "How often do you client events and what is that touchpoint process looks like?"
- "When's the last time you hosted a client appreciation event at a sporting event?"

Product Knowledge:
- "Where do you usually sit when you come to XYZ Park/Arena/Stadium?"
- "Who comes to the games with you?"
- "How familiar are you with our seating options?"

- "How many games do you usually attend per month?"
- "Where is your ideal seat at this venue?"

Premium Areas:
- "What are your thoughts on our premium experience?"
- "What do you know about the premium areas and its perks?"
- "When's the last you've sat and dined in our premium area?"
- "What do you enjoy most about the premium experience?"
- "If you were to get these seats, who would you typically invite or bring?"

Suites:
- "What would putting your top five clients, prospects, and salespeople in a suite together for three hours at the venue do for your business?"
- "How have you utilized premium seating at sporting events in the past?"
- "How would your top clients feel about being treated to an all-inclusive suite experience for a game this season?"
- "What do you know about our premium suites and their perks?"
- "What do you enjoy most about our premium suite experience?"

Follow-up:
- "What other questions can I answer for you?"

- "When should I expect an answer from you one way or the other?"
- "Who else will be making this decision with you?"
- "What do I need to do on my end to get this done today?"
- "On a scale of 1-10 how likely are you to move forward with these seats? What can I do to get you to a 10?"

Closing:
- "What credit card would you like to put this on?"
- "Which payment plan option will you be utilizing?"
- "Will you be using a Visa, MasterCard, or American Express?"
- "Which choice benefits do you want to add as part of your membership?"
- "Who else do you know that would be interested in joining our family?"

As you see, there are a lot of different open-ended questions that you can ask. Much like everything you do, take the time to practice and repeat these questions over and over until they become part of your everyday language.

1. Open ended questions all of the time. Hold yourself accountable.
2. Know these questions like the back of your hand.
3. Build relationships.

ASK FOR THE SALE

After you've built a solid relationship with the customer, it's time to ask for the sale. Many salespeople think that asking for the sale is the hardest part of the job. "I get nervous," some tell me. "I don't know if I would buy what I am selling," others say.

Guess what? If you can't ask for the sale, you will never make one.

One of the most important things in asking for the sale is making sure you have the right attitude going into the entire sales process. Do you believe in your product? Do you believe in yourself that you can sell to anyone? Do you know your entire sales process *cold*? In your sleep, can you walk through relationship building, asking open-ended questions, and ultimately identifying a product that fits their wants and needs?

Going into any sales call or appointment, be in the mindset that you have everything to gain and nothing to lose. The worst thing that can happen is you are told no. Simply going in with the attitude you are going to win will automatically raise your confidence level and lead to better outcomes.

In my opinion, asking for the sale is one of the easiest things to do if you have done all the other little things right. Did you go in with a pre-call objective? Did you build a relationship, use I/My's, ask the right questions, pump up a face-to-face meeting, etc.? Remember: people love to buy but hate to be sold to. If you put yourself in a position to be successful, there isn't much selling, as the customer can see the value proposition for themselves.

Throughout my time in this business, there are countless times that salespeople came back from an appointment and during the recap they would tell me that they didn't get around to asking the potential customer if they want to buy. WHAT?! WHY?! You spent so much time building a connection, learning about them, telling a bit about your product, why would you ever not ask for a commitment? That shouldn't even be an option—you have taken time out of their day, they have taken time out of yours, so now it's time to come to terms of if you are going to do business or not.

By the time you are getting ready to pitch a product, you should be in the process of assuming the sale. The assumptive close is a great tactic used to close a deal as you as the salesperson is assuming the prospect is agreeing to buy and you go straight into "What credit card would you like to use?". I know you have been taught to not assume things, but if you done everything right, you should assume the sale. At the end of the day, you are offering a great product.

5 Keys to asking for the close in the sports sales business is as follows:

1. Present the location and plan
2. List the top benefits (3 at the most)
3. Only the benefits that matter based upon what you have learned
4. Paint the Picture
5. Use "ONLY" and "JUST" when presenting the price
6. Say How cool is that? How Excited are you to join our family?
7. If they say yes, "Great! Let's take care of this now!"

That's the simple way of asking for the sale; there are obviously many other ways to ask for the sale, including some listed below. Again, I would encourage you to listen to your peers, read additional books/articles, and find which closing statements you feel most comfortable with and roll off your tongue the best.

- "It seems like the product is a good fit for you. What do you think?"
- "If we could find a way to deal with <OBJECTION>, would you join our family today?"
- "Taking all of your interests and needs into consideration, I think these two products would work best for you. Would you like to go with A or B?"
- "What do you say? How about you join our family today?"
- "Unless you have any more questions, I think we are ready to go ahead and lock these up."
- "How comfortable are you doing business with me today?"

When asking for the close, you may start hearing additional objections that may have never come up. Don't get discouraged; honestly this might be the way to get the potential customer to a yes or no. They may just be coming up with every reason under the sun that they can't do business that day because they may not be ready at this point. That's ok; get a yes or no, period point blank. A lot of times you will hear an objection that is easy to address, as you just may not have provided them enough details on the benefits/plan/package/etc. Clarity will help them get over the fence.

I hope by now its engrained in your head that to always ask for the sale no matter what. The second and last thing you always need to make sure you do is setup a definitive next step. When recapping an appointment with reps, I always ask them "What are the next steps?" or "When will the decision be made?" Too many times, salespeople reply "I told them I would follow up next week" or "I told them I would wait to hear from them." That immediately takes away any urgency or demand that you have created for your product.

At the end of each meeting or phone call, be sure to set a definitive time to reconnect and what the follow up will consist of. For example: "Great, glad to hear that you are interested. I am going to leave you with this benefit document, and I will call you on Friday at 3pm to lock in your seats!" This not only gives the exact time that you are calling, but again the assumptive close locks in your location. Here's another way: "Would you rather walk up to your seats or down to your seats? Let's go ahead and lock these up as the only thing that is going to change between now and Friday is your seat location!"

At the end of the day, the seats we are selling should be moving quickly, so getting decisions within 72 hours is key in our business. If the prospect says that time frame won't work, be sure to say, "Why don't you go ahead and get your calendar out and I will get mine; and I will send over a calendar invite with the exact time to finalize this deal?"

Do not leave that appointment or call without a definitive next step. You want to be elite in this business, elite sales professionals can build relationships, ask the right questions, ask for the sale, and set definitive next steps. No matter what type of lead you are talking to, asking for the sale won't change. Find a way to make it happen and get a yes or no!

1. Follow the entire sales process.
2. Use ONLY and JUST.
3. Definitive next steps.

CHAPTER 6

GROWING YOUR NETWORK

I accepted a role with the Miami Marlins with new owner-ship, and early on I realized I needed to have our team focus on building influencers within the community. Nurturing relationships and gaining referrals will go such a long way in growing your revenue streams. Many times you may go to an organization that doesn't have the best public percep-tion surrounding them so it's important to immerse your-self in the community to not only share your story but to also focus on the bigger opportunities at hand. Being able to sell to a business is such a huge opportunity as typically they don't care about wins and losses but just the overall experience and most importantly the value proposition that is provided. As you continue to grow in your career, you will start identifying businesses or business owners that are successful and applying some of their values and character-istics to your day to day.

As you become more experienced and successful, you will learn quickly that sales lead to more sales. In this chap-ter, I will show you how to leverage your current customers and find new business opportunities to create more sales.

REFERRALS

Anyone that has ever worked for me knows that one of my biggest pet peeves is not asking for referrals on every call. At the end of the year, when leaders look at sourcing campaigns, referrals are typically in the top 5. The only reason they aren't number 1 is because sales team members don't ask for them every time.

Why is that? Some common excuses are:

- "I forgot"
- "The customer needed to go."
- "I already set a meeting with them."
- "I was nervous they would get upset."

Guess what all of those reasons have in common? You. You just simply didn't do it, or you are overthinking the process and the simplicity of asking another question. I will say it until I am blue in the face: referrals are a huge part of our business and WILL separate you from the other competition. And the best part about it is that all you have to do is ASK.

In this business, you will make a lot of cold calls. How great is it to be able to make a lukewarm call? "The reason for my call today is because <NAME> gave me your information and said you would be the best person to speak to." Think about it – this makes our job so much easier, because now you have the credibility with the new customer because of how you received their information. Sales referrals help bridge the trust gap between you and the referred prospect. A Nielsen study recently said that people are four times more likely to buy when referred by a friend. The study also found that 92% of people trust referrals from people they know.

I will go out on a limb and say that sales members could hit their sales goal 90% of the time if they ask and receive referrals on a consistent basis. The main part of referrals is making sure you continue to keep your passion level high. Don't be afraid to offer rewards to customers who refer friends. Many apartment complexes will typically give you a free month's rent if you refer someone that signs a lease with them. I love free rent (who doesn't?), so I am going to tell everyone that has a pulse they should live in my building. If you can show value to the customer on why they should refer your business, they are more likely to provide you names/information.

Below is just a list of sample referral questions. It may seem a little intrusive to you, but just like any script I share in this book, this referral script has been around a long time and it works. Just use it!

If the customer purchased tickets:

"<NAME>, let me be the first to congratulate you and welcome you to the <XYZ Team> family! How does it feel? Well <CUSTOMER'S NAME> let me help you feel even better. The feedback we get from our fans is overwhelming. They tell us that they have much more fun at our games when they create their own mini section, surrounding themselves with their closest friends and family. So <CUSTOMER'S NAME>, of all your closest friends and family, who are the top 3 that you want sitting in your mini section? What are their cell phone numbers? What are their email addresses? What should I say when I introduce myself to them?"

If they say nobody...

"Well <CUSTOMER'S NAME>, a lot of our fans said that same thing until they posted a short message on their Facebook wall and were astounded by the results. They simply posted something like: Best day ever! I just bought season tickets for the XYZ team and my personal ticket team member <YOUR NAME> told me I could create my own mini section if my friends call within the next two days. So, come on! Join me and call <YOUR NAME> at xxx-xxx-xxxx or email at xxx@email.com."

If the customer didn't purchase tickets:

"<CUSTOMER'S NAME> It's clear that season tickets are not a fit, but maybe you can help me out."

Another great thing I do here is put together group outings at a discounted rate. I would love to get you a free ticket or help you get free tickets to a game. I will simply call your boss,

- "Where do you work?"
- "Where does your wife work?"
- "Who coordinates company outings? What's the best way to contact them?"
- "We have found that worship communities bring large groups to our games. Where do you worship?"
- "Who is your youth minister/adult director/singles director?"
- "What's the best way to contact them?"
- "Where do your children go to school?"
- "Who is the director of school activities? What's the best way to contact them?"

- "What adult sports leagues or organizations are you involved in? What leagues are your children involved in?"
- "We also have fantastic alumni nights. Where did you go to school? Who is the director of the alumni association?"
- "Who do you know that would be a good fit for XYZ team tickets?"

These referral scripts are pretty self-explanatory. The first and easiest one to ask is if the customer purchased, they obviously see the value in you and your product, so odds are they are in social circles that have similar interests. Let's be honest, who wouldn't want to go to games and sit around a bunch of people that they like? Always ask for multiples: if someone is willing to give you one name, they will probably give you more than one.

The end of the individual buyer script—once you either set the meeting or have been told no—is a great time to dive into the referral questions. If someone isn't agreeing to meet with you, this is probably the last time you will ever talk to them—so make sure you get the most out of the call. Don't give up and keep asking. What's the worst that can happen? They hang up on you. Ask referral questions until that happens.

If someone sets a meeting with you, they have already built enough trust and relationship with you that start asking the referral questions. Again, the worst that can happen is they say no, or they don't have time right now but at least it is in their mind. People that are legit prospects don't seem to mind talking about referrals. They see the value of your product, so they have no problem sharing it with friends.

The main thing with referrals is you have to keep the energy level up and the excitement of asking the questions. You will never get a referral if you are asking like you just broke your foot. Show the excitement over the phone and talk about how it could benefit them. It's an easy opportunity to get them a free ticket by connecting you to their company or organization.

Many of these referral questions can be asked during the entire conversation. If a customer says they want to go to more games but are so busy with work, you can say, "Oh, I understand. Where do you currently work?" You can then come in at the end when you start asking about referral questions with "I also work with a lot of groups in putting together special group outings. You mentioned you work at XYZ company; who should I reach out to there about employee outings?" Or, if the customer mentions that their daughter is very busy with playing basketball and soccer, you can say, "You had mentioned your daughter is involved in a lot of different leagues. We specialize in fundraising opportunities; what league is she involved with and who is in charge?"

As you can see, this is why referrals work so well. Most of the questions are easy and have already been given to you; you just need to ask for a contact. How big is social media nowadays? We already hit on the importance of your page but think about the value to you and your business if majority of your customers posted about their experience on their social platforms? You are getting free advertisement to everyone in their network. What does it hurt to ask?

- What is the best time to ask for referrals?

The best time to ask for referrals is while you are engaged in conversation. Many salespeople say "Well, I will wait until I meet with them in person to ask." Two thoughts to that: Unfortunately, not everyone you set a meeting will show up, so don't lose out on the opportunity. Secondly, by talking to them in advance about referrals, the customer has the opportunity to think about it prior to your in-person meeting.

- Is it possible to ask too many referral questions?

Customers will always tell you if they have to go, if you have asked too many questions, or if they don't have any more information for you. Don't overanalyze; let the customer dictate the question. As long as you are asking in the right way, you will never upset someone enough that they won't buy. If that is truly their excuse, then they weren't a legit buyer anyway.

- I received a referral from the customer, so I stopped asking.

No, no, no.... why would you do that? If a customer is willing to give you one referral, they are much more likely to get you 2 or 3 or 7. Keep asking, as they certainly see the value in you, your product, and what you are offering.

Referrals are key to your business and most importantly key to making more money. This should be the easiest thing you do in this business. Hold yourself accountable to doing it. It works, I promise.

1. Key to a successful career.
2. ASK every call, every time.
3. Warm calls are better than cold.

B2B OUTREACH

Pitching to businesses can be daunting, but the fundamentals are the same as any other prospective sale. In general, many inside sales teams will start out with individual buyer scripts and really train you up on getting a better understanding of what the phone calls, objections, appointments, and closings are going to look like.

It's easy for me to say now, but the key to being successful in the B2B landscape is to do the same thing you are doing for individual buyers. Why is it typically pretty easy to learn and adapt to the individual buyer script? It's because you ultimately just feel like you are talking to your mom, dad, or best friend about their experience and are finding ways to see if a partnership makes sense. You have spent your whole life talking to individuals, and that is in your comfort zone.

Businesses are more difficult because you haven't had any experience talking business with decision makers, and you will automatically think that businesses can spend more money with you so it just causes more anxiety going into. Prior to jumping into the business scripts, though, it's very important for you to get a better understanding of the business-to-business landscape. Thinking all of those things are not wrong which is why it is very important for you to study, practice, and really immerse yourself in the business community. You will be meeting with many decision makers that have been in business longer than you have been alive, so you have to find a way to come across as confident.

By selling B2B, you will make a lot more money, and your career trajectory will go a lot quicker. Many people who have left the industry just couldn't find a way to sell B2B, so this is the opportunity for you to have to really take your career to the next level. There is more to it than just practicing the script and assessing questions that can help lead you in the direction you want to take. Continue to focus on having that business state of mind, and, just like you should go into each and every outreach with a plan, take the time to build out what that may look like.

All business decision makers will do business differently so there is not one right approach that will sell every business that you speak with. The most important piece is going in with a consultative mindset. Don't go in with preconceived notions such as "they are a large company, therefore they should do a large employee outing," or "they make a lot of money so they should definitely buy a suite lease." Again, these decision makers have been through the dog and pony show of hearing from salespeople on all sides of their business. Final Decisions Makers (or FDMs) are going to see right through any bullshit that you try to present to them. However, FDMs do love to talk about themselves and their business. They always like to see ideas that can improve their business, which is where we come in.

You will see from the scripts and questions below, it's all about building relationships and finding ways to get the FDMs to think bigger and think outside of the box. The best scenario is as you are talking to a business, you set a meeting with the owner of the company, the head of sales, and the head of HR. First, the general rule of thumb when it comes to B2B is to have a minimum of 3 contacts for each business. The worst thing that can happen is you put all of your eggs in the basket of one person, and then they end up leaving the company and you have to start all over. Plus, if you meet with all of three of the heads of the company, you are now able to sell three different products—one that can help entertain customers on a consistent basis (season tickets), another to keep employee morale up (group outings), and another to entertain top executives and customers (suites). If you just met with one person in that company, you may walk away with a group outing or a season ticket purchase, but not all three. Think about it: companies have more money to spend, and if you can get multiple people involved you will get multiple entertainment budgets involved.

I could go on and on about B2B sales and different tips and tools to be successful. However, here I just want to provide you a quick overview so you can have some insight as you go into your interview or your first few months on the job. There are a lot of great B2B sales books, and I would highly recommend reading as many as you can to learn new styles and ultimately adapt to your strengths.

Typically, the first interaction you will have with a business is someone called the gatekeeper. A few pieces of advice on handling a gatekeeper:

- As always, be genuine and upfront. (They do this for a living so they can see the shady salespeople and the honest ones.)
- Take the time to build a relationship with them. (Many times, the gatekeepers are the right-hand people to

the FDMs or even a relative or close friend.)
- Ask for more information. (Who typically knows more about a company than the individual on the front line?)
- Remember them. (You will probably talk to them multiple times so remember their name, write them a card, go the extra step.)

Many times, gatekeepers will help lead you to a sale. I have even seen several that help make the decision as they are very close to the FDM. I promise you it's not going to help by trying to go around them all the time. They can be your inside source to getting a deal done.

1. Introduce yourself to the gatekeeper

"Good morning/good afternoon, my name is <YOUR NAME> and I am a corporate entertainment consultant with the front offices of the team and venue. I understand that <PROSPECT'S FIRST AND LAST NAME> is the final decision maker in regard to client entertainment and business growth at (your company). May I please speak to <PROSPECT'S FIRST NAME>? *or* Would you help me please? Who would be the final decision maker? "

If not told earlier...

"Oh, I am sorry! I introduced myself, but I didn't get your name...<GATEKEEPER'S FIRST NAME> it's nice to speak with you!"

What if they say, "He's not available right now"?

"<GATEKEEPER'S NAME>, I can appreciate that, you know his schedule better than I do, when would be a good time to call back?"

If the gatekeeper continues to tell you there is no such thing as good time (i.e., the FDM is in and out of the office all the time, they come and go as they please, etc.)

"<GATEKEEPER'S NAME>, what time does <FDM's NAME> begin or end his/her day? When is the best time to contact <FDM's NAME>, mornings or afternoons?"

"<GATEKEEPER'S NAME>, I really don't want to continue to bother you, if you were going to get a hold of him, when would you call <FDM's NAME>?"

If the gatekeeper says that no one at the company handles that...

"<GATEKEEPER'S NAME>, I can appreciate that, but the people who I normally deal with are the President, CEO, owners of the company...who would be in that position at the company?"

If the gatekeeper says that they don't do anything like that...

"<GATEKEEPER'S NAME>, I can certainly appreciate that as some of my best clients said the same exact thing before they saw the return on investment they received from our premium products, when is the best time to follow-up with <FDM'S NAME>?"

If the gatekeeper sends you to voicemail....

"<GATEKEEPER'S NAME>, I just spoke with you as you sent me to <FDM'S NAME>'s voicemail. I am actually going to be in meetings the rest of the day and I'd hate to miss his/her call, when is the best time for me to contact <FDM'S NAME>?"

When you go to voicemail, listen for tips. What do they refer to themselves as, cell phone, title, etc. Use this going into next call.

Additional questions to ask the gatekeeper to determine their viability as a prospect...

"<GATEKEEPER'S NAME>, well tell me this, who handles your other sports tickets with the company?"

"What exactly is ABC company? Who are your clients?"

"When is the last time you made it out to the venue?"

"When is the last time the company held an outing?"

"How big of a sports fan is <FDM'S NAME>?"

"Who is the biggest sports fan in the company?"

"How many salespeople do you have?"

At this point you will have built a great relationship with the gatekeeper and obtained a lot of great information about the company. Again, this may have occurred over multiple calls. Now it's time to talk to the FDM. No different than the individual buyer script, you have 10 seconds to make an impact. Go in with passion and energy and get to the point.

The main thing on the B2B end is you want to meet face-to-face. Odds are if you get through to the FDM on a phone call, you have probably caught them in between meetings or tasks and they probably aren't going to have the time to be able to dive into their business. As you will see in the script, it's important to say who you are, provide a benefit statement, and then ask to meet with them face to face at their office (their comfort zone). By going out to their office, it's going to be much easier to find a way to meet the 3 different contacts as well as seeing more about their business firsthand.

The remainder of the business script will hopefully provide some reference to additional assessing questions and relationship builders that you can utilize. Be sure to take the time to continue to dive into the B2B questions, role play with your leaders/peers, and continue to find a way to be successful in this landscape, as this will help separate you from your competition.

2. Talking to the FDM

"Hi <NAME THE PROSPECT USED WHEN AN-SWERING>! My name is <YOUR NAME> with the team and venue and we partner with <ABC> company and I wanted to discuss with you ways I can assist in increasing revenue and assist in customer and employee retention."

Ask for the meeting...

"My out of office days are typically Tuesday's and Thursday's. How about I swing by your office next Tuesday at 10am and we can meet to discuss if you could utilize us much like <ABC> company."

Once you set the meeting...

"I look forward to meeting with you. What other companies are in your building/office park that I could call and meet with after I meet with you?"

Additional questions to engage the decision maker....

"Some of my top clients currently have 4 seats and utilize them to help differentiate themselves from the competition. How are you differentiating yourself from the top competition? How are you currently entertaining your top clients?"

- "How important is maintaining your top relationships? What are you currently doing to maintain those top relationships?"

  - *If YES to dinner/golf/entertainment.....*
    - "How successful has it been?"
    - "How often do you entertain on a monthly basis?"
    - "Who usually does the entertaining for you?"
    - "How often do you do dinners/golf?

Where do you generally go?"
  ▷ "What has made these successful?"
  ▷ "What other ways are you currently entertaining your top clients?"

► *If YES to other sports.....*
  ▷ "How successful have those been?"
  ▷ "How do you utilize those tickets?"
  ▷ "Who usually does the entertaining for you?"
  ▷ "How many seats do you have?"
  ▷ "How many games per month do you attend?"
  ▷ "What has made those tickets a success?"

- "What other forms of client entertainment do you currently use?"
- "How are you incentivizing your top employees?"
- "A lot of my best clients use referrals to grow, what have you done in the past to ensure that you maintain those top relationships so that they'll continue to send referrals your way?"
- "How familiar are you with our upscale and affordable client entertainment options?"

Being able to have the consultative mindset as you go into business calls is very important because at the end of the day, you need to be able to find the right value proposition. Similar to the appointment agenda, below is a list of thought provoking phrases, questions, or key comments that you can discuss to help showcase the opportunity you are providing by building a partnership.

*Tell me more about your business
*It will pay for itself over and over again with each client! We are here to compliment your current entertainment options.

Comments
- Face time is exactly what we have here
- Not trying to replace, we are trying to compliment
- Buyer Beware
- You owe it to yourself
- It would give you another outlet

Keys
- Help Grow the Business
- Increase Customer Loyalty
- Reduce Costs
- Improve Productivity
- Gain a competitive advantage

INTRODUCTION QUESTIONS

"Tell me a little bit more about yourself and your business?"
- A good conversation starter; gets them talking more about the business.
- Here you are able to break beyond the information on their website and get into the meat and bones of what they do.
- Also, this can lead you into the other relevant topics below.

SALES AND RENEWAL PROCESS QUESTIONS

"How does your company generate new business?"
- The first questions that help us lean about their

company's sales process.
- Our objective is to decipher where we can insert our product into their process to make them successful.

"How many salespeople do you have?"
- Helps us get the size and scope of the organization.
- Can be used in tangent with other questions to determine how large of a plan and how many seats they need.
- Answer can be used to overcome usage and # of ticket objections.

"When do you renew your clients? How do you renew your business?"
- Prospects often overlook the fact that tickets can be used in their renewal process as well as when bringing in a new customer.
- Our objective is to decipher where we can insert our product into their process to make them successful.

"How important is maintaining relationships? Why? How do you currently do that? What has been most successful?"

Gauge the importance of relationship building. Most people will say it's very important.

Another way to ask is, "On a scale of 1 to 10, how important is it to maintain relationships in your business?

CUSTOMER INFORMATION

"Who are your key customers?"
- Tell us who they're doing business with currently. Once we know who these businesses are, reference them specifically as opposed to the generic "customers" or "clients" when relevant in the conversation.
- The logical question after this is how many other customers to you currently work with?
- How many accounts do you have?
- Use information to determine how many seats will be needed for the customer

"What is your average sale?"
- Helps determine the value of each customer.
- Information learned will help us determine what product could be the best fit.
- What you learn here could help overcome the price objection. i.e. "I can appreciate that, but the return on investment is substantial. Based on what we've discussed, with x opportunities to entertain your prospects with this option, if you were to convert X of these prospects into customers you would easily recoup the costs of this investment. We're only looking at $$$$ per a seat, so what do you say, let's lock these up?"

"What's your average profit?"
- How much of the revenue is the prospect taking home? Not a key question, but one that you could ask.

PAST TREND QUESTIONS

"What type of entertainment have you done in the past?"

- Depending on the sale of entertainment that they have done in the past it will help us determine what kind of experience they are suited for with us. i.e.
- If they are used to very upscale dinners or have a suite elsewhere, at minimum they are a fit for a club seat product.
- If they've only done hunting and other experiences that cost no more than $40 per person, they're likely not the best fit for premium seats.

"How has that worked in the past? What made it successful?

- Gets the customer talking about what was successful and what wasn't about their past experiences.
- Helps us determine what experiences we have to offer that are important to highlight or downplay based upon their response.

"How often do you entertain?"

- Frequency of current entertainment trends helps us determine what kind of a plan they would be a fit for. For example, if a company is entertaining 3 or 4 times a month and has only two employees they aren't a fit for full suite. If a company entertains 10 to 12 times a month, an 11-game plan would not be the plan to start with.

EMPLOYEE & INCENTIVE QUESTIONS

"How many employees do you have? What are you currently doing for employee outings?"

- A key question that can be used to overcome usage issues.
- Identifying potential outings.

"What types of incentives do you usually give your top producers?"

- A key question that can be used to overcome usage issues, i.e. "One of my best customers actually uses a portion of their tickets to recognize someone on their team and drive behavior. They once gave out tickets to the first employee that arrived for work. The next day, there were a number of other employees who got to work earlier!"

"How often would you utilize tickets from a personal perspective?"

- Great question to ask small to mid-range business owners that have or may have issues with ticket usage.

PRESENTATION QUESTION

"How familiar are you with our premium areas?"

- A great way to transition into a presentation of the club products that we have to offer.
- If they are familiar and tried it out get them talking about their experiences before going into details.

Finally, when meeting with the multiple different decision makers; be sure to find out as much detail and information as possible. Utilize "Tell Me More" and always provide a thought-provoking solution that could benefit them. The walk up the stairs can be very easy with FDMs as long as you ask the right questions.

1. B2B can accelerate your career.
2. Research each and every person you will be meeting with.
3. Three sources of contact with each company.

GROUP SALES

Group sales calls can really tie into both an individual buyer as well as a business. There are a wide variety of calls that will either be groups or turn into a potential group sale and that is why it is key to be a full-menu consultant. We just discussed businesses, every business should have a discussion about an employee outing or an event for all of their customers. If you think about calling a youth fellowship group; you are probably going to talk to the youth pastor/ priest who is running the group but also is a parent of a kid that is in the organization. To ramp up the excitement on that end, not only are you able to talk about their individual experiences but also understand their group initiatives. You will see that all the group sales script is very similar to a business as you may come across a gatekeeper and you will really need to assess and understand what their group initiatives and priorities are. In this example, calling a fellowship organization can lead you down several group possibilities including discussions with the head pastor, youth minister, choir director, or men's and women's director. Like any call, find as many contacts as you can and focus on asking the right thought provoking questions.

1. Introduce yourself to the gatekeeper

"Good morning/good afternoon, my name is _____ and I am a group entertainment consultant with the front offices of the venue and team. Would you help me please? I understand that <PROSPECT'S FIRST AND LAST NAME> is in charge of group outings at the organization. May I speak to <PROSPECT'S FIRST NAME>?"

If not told earlier...

"Oh, I am sorry! I introduced myself, but I didn't get your name...<GATEKEEPER'S NAME> it's nice to speak with you!"

No Voicemail...

"I'm going to be in and out of the office and I would really hate to miss their call. When would be the best time to reach him/her?"

"Thanks so much <GATEKEEPER'S FIRST NAME>, you've been a huge help! I am ready to be transferred."

2. Introduce yourself to the prospect

"Hi <NAME HE/SHE USED WHEN ANSWER-ING>! My name is <YOUR NAME> and I am a group entertainment consultant with venue and team. I specialize in working with different churches to create exciting and affordable group outings and I am curious, what type of group activities does your church [youth, choir, congregation] currently do?"

- "How often do you have these activities?"
- "How many people attend these events?"
- "How big is your organization?"
- "Who attends the events?" (families, friends, congregation, etc.)
- "How successful have these group outings been?"
- "What made these groups outings so successful?"
- "What types of sports outings have you done in the past?"
- "How do you communicate these events?" (internet, email, flyers, etc.)
- "If you could plan a perfect event at the venue, what would that look like?"
- "How familiar are you with the teams' group sales programs?"

"<PROSPECT'S FIRST NAME>, this is the perfect time for us to be having this conversation because we've just created several extraordinary affordable group outing options. <PROSPECT'S FIRST NAME>, I'd love to host you for a VIP tour of the venue to show you some of the experience packages we have available. How does <DAY> and <TIME> sound?"

No matter what type of call you are making, your main objective is to find a way to meet face-to-face. Many times, similar to the business script, the call will go back and forth between individual and business/group conversation. It is very important that you really practice and understand any and all questions for all of the scripts because you never know what the conversation may turn into.

These are 3 of the basic scripts and you will be given plenty more depending on calls (cancelled plan, renewal, church, non-profit, events, etc.). As a reminder, internalize them and make them your own. Don't let this be the last time you read the last few chapters. Go back and read them to your friends/family. Then read them in front of a mirror. Take the time to study, prepare, and be ready to dominate your day. Trust me—they work.

1. Understand the type of group they are and what their goals are.
2. Communication.
3. Think BIG.

CHAPTER 7

STRATEGIES FOR CONTINUED SUCCESS

I have discussed several times in this book about the importance of working with the right people and the right opportunity. One of my first bosses and mentors, Brendan Donohue, was working at the NBA League Office in a division call Team Marketing Business Operations. He gave me a call and wanted me to join to help oversee ticketing for all NBA, WNBA, and G-League teams by traveling around each week to new markets and meeting with teams, sharing best practices, and ultimately finding ways to be successful. Throughout this experience, I was able to meet a lot of great people, see many different perspectives, understand the struggles from different markets, and most importantly catch a glimpse of what elite people in this business were focusing on a daily basis. At the end of the day, it call comes down to having that "Win" mentality and finding ways to win every minute you are perfecting your craft.

In this final chapter, I will leave you with some tips and best practices for taking your career to the next level.

FIND UNIQUE WAYS TO REACH OUT

As I have discussed evolving with the business and the world around us; evolving in the marketplace is also very important. When I first started in the business, it was 99% phone calls as text messaging, emails, or LinkedIn wasn't that popular. I remember sitting in the office on Friday nights waiting for faxes to come through to receive an order. When was the last time (if ever) did you send a fax?

The one constant in this world is change and that can be both positive and negative but if you can't adapt to change and the surroundings around you, you will get passed especially in this business. Anyone that knows me knows how important I believe phone calls are in this business, but I also want you to be able to think outside the box in order to get in touch with decision makers. What I mean by this is, think about all of the possible ways that you can communicate with someone, such as:

- Phone call
- Email
- LinkedIn
- Handwritten card
- Drop by at their office

Not every potential customer will be the same—some you may connect with on the first call, some may take 8 calls, and some may never answer the phone. In this business, it's a waste of your time if you aren't doing something different to try to connect with someone, which hopefully will lead to a sale.

With the five different ways to connect above, why not

try each method out with each lead that you have? For example: If you have 50 leads, start 10 with a phone call, 10 with an email, 10 with a LinkedIn Message, 10 with a handwritten card, and 10 by dropping by their office. What's the worst that can happen? You identify which outreach method works best for you to get the most face-to-face meetings. Once you start this process, be sure to track it so you know what has been successful, but more importantly what the follow up process looks like. If the first 10 you start with a phone call, a few days later send them a LinkedIn message, followed by a handwritten card, and then an email. Repeat this process a few times (my general rule of thumb is to make 8 types of outreach before closing out the lead and moving on) and be creative in the outreach messages.

When it comes to being successful in this business and your city's marketplace; you want to get your name out as much as possible. You never know whose hands a business card, a note, or an email may end up in. Make it rain in the marketplace where everyone knows who you are and that you can be their inside source for the team.

Many teams will host sales events, so be sure to think outside the box with those as well. Start with a phone call talking about the event, follow it up with an email invitation with specifics, send a handwritten note with your business card, send a calendar invite, and follow it up the day before with a hype call. A hype call is not a confirmation, but a call delivered with passion and excitement leading the potential customer to also be excited and ready to join the family.

Evolve in this business, take risks, think outside the box, and go outside your comfort zone. Years ago, nobody would have dreamed to send a credit card number via text, but now it happens consistently. The worst thing that can happen with any of this is someone tells you please don't reach out that way. Push yourself to be elite!

1. Evolve your outreach tactics.
2. Change up your methods consistently.
3. Go out of your comfort zone.

TIME MANAGEMENT

As we have discussed, this business is very difficult in a lot of ways, but I think the biggest challenge many sales professionals have is time management. As you can imagine, there are a variety of tasks on your plate each and every day from internal meetings, phone calls, prospecting, appointments, follow ups, etc. Being able to be efficient and effective every day is vitally important to having success in your career.

Every day is different, and the beauty of this business is you will truly have the autonomy to run your own day. At the end of each day, if you can look yourself in the mirror and say you gave it your all, that is a success. If you can figure out to be efficient every day, you won't have to worry about a leader being all in your business. They will trust that you are doing the right things to be successful.

In the book *7 Habits of Highly Effective People,* author Stephen R. Covey breaks down time management into four quadrants: urgent, not urgent, important, and not important. In general, this is a very good book and I would recommend reading it in its entirety, but here I want to focus on this idea of quadrants. Breaking up the day helps you to focus on building capabilities, maximizing opportunities, and risk management. Many of the tasks you will be given in your career aren't necessarily urgent, but they are important and those are the ones you should always plan to do. The challenge I see in sales professionals is when they spend way too much time working on items that aren't urgent or very important.

My advice on time management is to make sure you are in control of your own schedule. I know you may be thinking, "But what if my boss tells me to do something?" I am not saying you won't have tasks that are important, but make sure that you are building out your schedule on a consistent basis. Prior to you leaving for the day, you should put together a checklist that details out what goals you have for tomorrow. Take time to identify and schedule activities around your most important goals. Try for a 70/30 split; plan 70% of your day around appointments and tasks that need to be completed and leave 30% of your day open and unplanned. This will always give you the opportunity to respond to customer requests, make new outreach, or be able to be nimble if a customer says they can meet that day.

Like anything in life, you should set goals for managing your time and controlling your day. The first step of that is realizing what is important and be sure to set your day accordingly. Your immediate and/or end goal needs to be in mind when scheduling. Always remember that the current task that you are focusing on is going to affect your short- and long-term goals you have set for the day/week.

At the end of the day, sales is a numbers game. When thinking about the numbers game, it really breaks down to the APS system. Appointments=Prospects=Sales! Take a look at some easy math below:

- If you make 75 calls a day, **50** of those should be NEW calls to people you haven't yet spoken to
- Of these NEW calls, you will probably only talk to **20** of them
- Of these you talk to, you should set a minimum of **2** appointments per day
- What's your NO quota: **Every 10 no's = 1 yes**
- That leaves you with **10** appointments set per week
- Of these set appointments, you will only complete **6** of them
- What's your NO quota: About every appointment that doesn't show the next one will
- Of these completed appointments, you will only close **2** of them
- What's your NO quota: **Every 3 no's = 1 yes**
- Let's say on average, each of these sales is worth $3,000. That means you are adding another **$6,000** of revenue per week and another **$24,000** of revenue per month on top of the sales that will naturally flow in. Now we are talking real money!

This is the difference between average salespeople and great salespeople. Consistent effort always brings consistent results. Managing your time effectively can mean more money.

One of the biggest challenges of time management is how to manage interruptions. The main way that I manage interruptions is to set goals and hold myself accountable to them, but here are a few other ideas:

1. Turn off notifications (set out of office email/voice-mail)

2. Prioritize all of the things that are currently on your plate
3. Find out what is most important to you
4. Prioritize your number of touches
5. Challenge each other. Let people know what distracts you. Put something on your desk.
6. Be self-aware. Know what is/is not a distraction to you. Write down what distracts you and be aware of disruptions
7. Hold yourself accountable and be realistic about what keeps you from focusing on work
8. Schedule time to be away from your desk to avoid going stir crazy. Walk around the venue to clear your head. Maximize the time that you are at your desk
9. Plan your day ahead of time. Early Monday morning to set up the upcoming week or stay Friday afternoon to plan the following week.
10. Use your mornings productively
11. PLAN! PLAN! PLAN!

As you look at time management as a whole, it's important to take a deep dive into your day to day and figure out what is important and urgent. Set expectations for yourself each day and hold yourself accountable. Don't be afraid to say no. If it's not urgent or important, why are you spending time doing it? Control your own day!

1. Be efficient and effective every day.
2. You control your own schedule.
3. Manage interruptions.

PIPELINE

If you have had a relative or friend that has had a career in sales, many times you will hear them talking about their pipeline and how strong it may be. Pipelines are very important in this business for multiple reasons. One, you as the sales professional should always know what is in your pipeline to ensure that you are tracking your sales goals. Second, your boss will have their own projections for your sales growth, so having a strong pipeline can help you deflect criticism during a slow period.

To start building your pipeline, you must have a live sales opportunity that has a discrete beginning and end and multiple stages in between. When you join a team, there will be multiple ways for leaders to look at pipelines and many times they will be built out in your database system. I don't believe there is a right or wrong way, but I typically look at pipelines as four different stages:

- **Suspects** – people that you have an initial discussion with that was positive, someone that you have sent some information over to
- **Prospects** – people that you have an in-depth conversation with, someone that you have an appointment set with
- **Qualified Opportunities** – people that you have had an appointment with or someone that you have an in-depth conversation with, and you are expecting to close within the month
- **Closeable Opportunities** – people that you have had an appointment with and it's very promising that you

will close in the next few weeks, waiting on a check or for them to get it ok'd but it's going to come in

I always like to compare pipelines and the stages to a sporting field or court. If you think about baseball; first base is stage 1, second base is stage 2, third is stage 3, and finally scoring a run at home is stage 4. A basketball court can be broken down into inbounding the ball for stage 1; getting to half court for stage 2, starting a play at your own three-point line for stage 3, and slamming it home for a score in stage 4. When you take a look at the dugout or bench respectively for each of these, that is where you should plus in your new prospects. If you are going to have a really strong pipeline; you should be putting in 10 new prospects every single day. You should never have something in the pipeline longer than 45 days. I am not saying it's completely dead, but a pipeline should be something that is realistically closing in that timeframe.

I have broken down the areas below in regards to the field:

- **1st Base** - (Connected) Have an appointment (leave in pipeline a max of 14 days)
- **2nd Base** – (Interested) They need what you have, there is urgency and you have shown movement on the field (max of 7-10 days)
- **3rd Base** – (Sale Pending) The prospect is completely qualified to do business with you, and you are completely qualified to do business with the prospect (72 hours, max of 7 days)
- **Home Run** – (Won) You have presented the information, appropriate for the customer, and they

have made a decision to buy from you (max of 72 hours)

As you continue to get better and better at managing your pipeline, there are 3 big metrics that leaders look for in pipelines: size, contents, and progress.

Size breaks down into what is the pipeline growth over time and what is the total pipeline in both revenue and volume. The size of your pipeline should be a minimum of 4X of what your goal is. If you need to make it bigger, make more calls, set more appointments, and get more prospects and referrals.

Contents are what is the revenue by pipeline stage and revenue by sales cycle. The contents of a pipeline are gaining new opportunities: what is the quality of opportunities and what are the different lead sources you are focusing on. Think about how you can gain new prospects, attend more meetings, or focus on new campaigns.

And finally, progress is determined by the sales cycle length, percentage of deals advanced by stage, and what is the actual closing percentage of forecasted deals. This really comes down the percentage by each stage. If your pipeline mainly consists of people on first base (suspects), then your pipeline isn't going to be very strong in the next few weeks as none of those are likely to close. A very strong pipeline has an equal percentage across all four stages.

Be realistic about your pipeline. Like anything in this business, be honest and truthful to yourself on what can truly come in and what is just fluff. Having fluff in your pipeline helps nobody; people put fluff in because they realize they haven't done enough to be successful. Great leaders will see right through it.

The best leaders will continue to help you become an expert at managing your pipeline. Here are 5 ways to manage your pipeline:

1. Start with clear definitions and next steps by stage
2. Use a consistent tool – CRM
3. Develop a discipline for adding new prospects daily – no excuses
4. Conduct a weekly pipeline review for next steps (both with leader and by yourself)
5. Schedule daily follow-up calls to past clients and previous prospects
6. A quick exercise for you to always do to see the health of your pipeline is to do simple math to identify your close rate and plug that in to see what your target pipeline size needs to be.

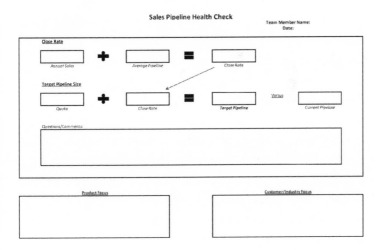

In this example, you will divide your annual sales by your average pipeline to get your close rate. You will then take your sales goal and divide that by your close rate to get your target pipeline. I would recommend doing this in two ways both your yearly goal as well as your monthly goal. Now like anything in this business, find a way to hold yourself accountable to managing a healthy pipeline.

1. Be honest about your pipeline.
2. Focus on consistent movement.
3. Hold yourself accountable to having a healthy pipeline.

CAREER GROWTH/MANAGING UP NOT SUCKING UP
The question I have received the most throughout my career is: What's the different between managing up versus sucking up?

The difference is huge. As I discussed earlier in the book, it's very important to make decisions where career growth is important. At the end of the day, you don't want to, and you can't be in entry-level sales your entire career. The teams that have great career development programs are the ones you want to stick with. I am excited to say that I think our business has really evolved over the last decade and there are a lot of great programs to start your career. The best way to grow your career is to put yourself in a good position. Good things happen to good people.

Managing up is key to our business, and it is a big difference from sucking up. Early on the easiest way to manage up is to do the little things right all the time. Make sure that you are on time, that you act in a professional manner all the time, and most importantly that you are making a name for yourself. What's the best way to get the attention from the President or VP of Sales? Lead in production! That can be as easy as winning the hustle board every week, busting your tail at sales events, and finding new ways to be successful.

Find ways to manage up internally by picking the brains of successful people around you. Early on in your career, find some time to meet one on one with the other leaders in the departments. Ask thought provoking questions very similar to some of the interview questions you may have already asked. Ask them when they were in your shoes, what did they do to be successful? Find individual time with top salespeople in your organization as well. Keep pushing to find ways to evolve and ultimately compete at the highest level and be the #1 salesperson in the company regardless of department or tenure. Be yourself in these meetings, show your personality, send a thank you, and start implementing things that you have learned to show that you listened and truly appreciate their time.

These are all little ways to always manage up, but the easiest way to do that is to have people talking about you in a positive manner at all times. "Wow that person set a lot of appointments." "Crazy how they are always at the top of the hustle and sales board." By doing the little things right, people will see the success you are having and that will help your career. No different than when you were first interviewing for a career, put yourself in a position that you have the ability to make the decision on what is next. That could be as simple as getting promoted from entry-level sales to Account Executive level. Down the road, it may be making the decision to take another opportunity in a leadership role.

As you continue on in your career, you will see sales professionals that have stayed at the same place their entire career or people that have worked for several different teams. No way is the right way or wrong way. Ultimately put yourself in a position to be able to make the best decision for you and your family. I was always able to move for promotion opportunities and work alongside some really great people, and that has helped me continue to evolve my career. I get excited looking back on my career and seeing all of the people I was able to work with and how it has developed me into the leader and sales professional that I am in today.

1. Put yourself in a good position by doing the little things right.
2. Find time with leaders and top individuals to pick their brains.
3. Learn from everyone both good and bad.

CONTINUOUS EDUCATION

I know by the name of this section, this is probably not going to intrigue too many of you. Most of you are either finishing school or have just finished. By continuous education, though, I am not saying you have to go back to school. When I think of continuous education, I want you to focus on how you are going to continue to evolve and get better every single day. You need to invest in yourself to be elite in this business.

Continuous education can be a wide variety of items that are very simple to do, and you will learn a lot. It all comes down to the one thing that we have continued to talk about: Are you willing to put the effort in?

Read

I am not here to tell you that you should read one book a week or 20 books a year, but at least try to read one book a month. Read one chapter every night before bed or right away in the morning; you will be surprised how easy is it to power through books. Early on in my career, I really dove into sales books, trying to understand how I could continuously improve my craft. As I have gotten older, I have started to read more business books. I always tell people that when you read a book, don't worry about trying to take something out of each chapter. If you can take even one thing out of an entire book and apply it to your day, you will be more successful.

Another quick and easy method is to subscribe to email newsletters on sales and business. These are typically quick reads that will probably take 10 minutes, but they can offer valuable insights into what others in the business and sales world are hearing and focusing on. Within many of these business articles, you will also see business trends, which helps as you continue to focus more and more on B2B sales.

Listen to Podcasts

How long is your drive to work? Since you are not going to the venue today to play a sport, you probably don't need to worry about listening to your pump-up music. Why not take the 15 minutes or so and listen to a sales/business podcast to get your mind thinking? Focus on the pump-up music as you drive home after you just closed a few big deals. Similar to books, try to take something out of it that you can apply to your day. In this day and age, there are so many different podcasts to choose from. I am not a big believer in telling you which ones to listen to or even which books to read; try several out and find ones that intrigue you. *I hear "52 Weeks of Hustle" is pretty good!*

Reach out to colleagues/mentors

Similar to your ride in or ride home, why not pick two days a week that you are going to call a mentor or someone else in the business to pick their brain and see how they are approaching similar topics? If you don't have a mentor, ask your leader to make introductions to other sales professionals in similar roles in other markets. Some of my best friends in the business I have never worked with but have known my entire career, as we constantly stay in contact and strive to make each other better. I promise you that if you are struggling at something in the sales world, odds are someone else has similar struggles. Try talking through solutions together. It never hurts to reach out to your peers, as you never know who you will end up working alongside one day.

At the end of the day, my hope is that you want to be a rockstar in the business so find ways to get better each and every day. The one constant in this world is change; so be prepared for it and find a way to win each and every day!

1. Find a way to educate yourself each week.
2. Apply any education you receive to your day.
3. Be prepared for change.

OVERCOMING STRUGGLES

In this business, you are going to have bad days. Full transparency: there are going to be days that you just want to quit. There isn't going to be much I can say that will help with that outside of the fact that it happens to the best sales professionals in the world. Remember, we aren't selling a necessity; we are selling an experience. That is always going to be an uphill climb.

Dealing with stress in general is a hard thing to overcome, and in this business you will have a lot of stress. You may start off really slow and not have many sales, so you start second guessing everything you are doing. You may start off really well and then hit a sales wall, not making any sales for a few weeks. Again, this is going to happen to everyone, so don't try to ride the highs too high or the lows too low. If you don't get stressed out if you have a week of no sales, limited appointments, and a ton of hangs up, then this business may not be for you. By not getting stressed, that probably means you aren't really bought into this.

Getting exposure to sales early on in your life or in college is key to figuring out if you can handle this. I have seen people that have never had any sales experience, rarely dealt with rejection their entire life, and then get into this business. Unfortunately, I have seen a lot of people self-select out of the business once the going gets tough.

There are a lot of times that you will have to deal with stress both personally and professionally. Stress could come from not making enough money, not being around friends and family, or working so many hours that you don't have a great work/life balance. The money situation will always come up; you can easily go get another job that you will work less hours, have more free time, and make more money, but the challenge will be whether you going to be passionate enough about that specific job.

I am not going to try to be your parents, but when it comes to money you need to make sure you are smart with it. I realize when you first get out of college, you probably don't have a ton of money and you are going to have student loans, rent, bills, etc. to pay for. Going to happy hours 3 nights a week probably isn't the best thing for you to be doing right now. What I can tell you about money is I have never heard of a team that will cap your commissions or limit the amount of money you will make. The beauty of being in sales is the more you sell, the more money you will make! I promise you by having a long career in this business, you will find a way to make more money than you have dreamed of. At that point, you can go to more happy hours and buy nicer things.

I have always told people I am not the best to talk to about a work/life balance as I have never quite figured it out, but I would tell you that it's going to be crucial to staying in this business a long time. There are going to be days that you are in the office at 7am and you won't leave until 11pm, and you do it all over again the next day. That's this business. My hope is you see that where you work is a place that brings a lot of people together. Think about it: being at a professional sports event is your job!

When confronting the stress of this job, my best advice is similar to what we discussed earlier about time management; find ways to manage your own day and find ways to make yourself productive in your personal life. There are many times that you will become stressed in this business, whether it be the actual work or not feeling like you have a life. Find ways to have that balance and always remember that the effort you put in now will pay dividends in your career and your personal life.

1. You will have slow and rough weeks.
2. Find ways to deal with stress.
3. Focus on a work/life balance.

ENJOY THE JOURNEY

At the end of the day, do things the right way and put yourself in a position to enjoy the journey. You will hear from a lot of leaders that this business is a marathon not a sprint, and they are absolutely right.

Too many sales professionals ride the rollercoaster, and they end up struggling or ultimately out of the business. You have to continue to figure out ways to not ride the highs too high or the lows too low. The most successful person is not the person that makes the first sale or is #1 on the board after a few months. The successful people are the ones that are constantly putting themselves in a position to be successful over the long haul.

It was hard for me to see the marathon part when I first got into the business because I wanted to be #1 and I wanted to get promoted and then get the title. As I spent more time in the business, I have learned that title, money, and responsibility will follow as long as you are around the right people and continue to put yourself in a position to be successful.

This business is a lot of fun, at the end of the day you are working for a professional sports franchise. You are literally getting paid to work and watch the greatest athletes in the world. You will continually be asked by friends/family/acquaintances what it is like to work in sports, and you will always be the center of conversations. Yes, I realize some of your family may not have a clue to what you do, so it will require a lot of explanation. That is no different from how you want the customer to talk about themselves, though; you will want to do that as well because you are so passionate about your craft and business.

No offense to anyone that does this, but you aren't selling vacuum cleaners. I own a Dyson vacuum and I love it but thankfully I don't have to find the passion to sell it every day. No matter how stressful the job may feel or the long hours you put in, it's important to keep your perspective and understand that we are in the business of experience and the business of fun! After all, your friends that are doctors aren't typically going to sit around with a few drinks and talk about the surgeries they just performed.

You are going to meet a lot of great people that will become your best friends and you will be able to see and be a part of a lot of exciting events. You will become family with the people you work with and more often than not; you are spending more time with them than you own family. You will train together, work alongside other in a very small area, work events together, hang out together, and often live together. Take these friendships and continue to find ways to challenge yourself with each of these as well.

Within this journey, you are going to come across peers that you may not like or trust, leaders that you don't respect, and many other things that may be required that you don't appreciate. However, my best advice is learn from every experience you are in. One day when you become a leader, you will be able to hire the people that you want to build a team around and hope you learned the do's and don'ts of being a great leader. You may come across leaders that you believe are micromanaging you. At times, they probably are and that is their job. Good leaders do everything they can to provide you the best training, sales techniques, the resources, the budget, and a lot of time and effort to help you become an elite seller and individual in this business. To accomplish this, the leader needs to be near you, watch you, listen to you, study you, and find ways to continually help you.

Many people in this business won't like the idea of being held accountable to everything they do. Guess what? It doesn't matter how long you have been in this business; you will be held accountable to everything you do. Sales is a numbers game, and great leaders will manage you to numbers. It will be a requirement to hit them on a consistent basis.

As we discuss numbers, you will continually see the people that you started with or have worked with move out of the roles. The one constant in this business is change which we have discussed previously but also with personnel. Some may quit early on as it's just not what they thought it would be or they just couldn't handle the pressure. Some may be asked to move on because of low productivity; some may leave on their own to take more guaranteed money; others may leave for promotions, which is one of the best things to see across the industry.

Finally, when you first start, you will not make a lot of money – period. It will be a low salary to start and all of the upside will be based on how you do. Budgeting is going to have to be something you prioritize and identify what is most important. This is a marathon, not a sprint, so you may not start out by making six figures, but it is very possible to do quickly I promise you—you can make a lot more money than you ever dreamed of, but you will have to put the time and effort into it.

There are going to be a lot of positives and some negatives in this business, and my hope is that you will continue to see the opportunity ahead of you and turn all of the negatives into opportunities. Never forget the excitement that you had when it came to interview at the team, your first day of work, or your first sale. Keep the passion and excitement every day and you will have a long career in this business. I wouldn't trade anything I have learned or went through in the world. Enjoy the journey!

1. This business is a lot of fun!
2. Marathon not a sprint.
3. Pinch yourself every once in a while and remember what you are doing for a living.

DO YOU WANT TO BE THE BEST?

As you continue you on in your career, you need to make sure you are striving to get better every single day. At the end of the day, you should ask yourself "Did I give it my all?" If your answer is no, you need to hold yourself accountable and make sure you come back the next day ready to go and be sure to give 110%.

"Why Do I Work in Sports Sales?" – I am sure you have asked yourself this or have been asked this. What is your answer? I bet 90% of you would say because you are passionate about sports, sales, and being a part of the environment. This is an industry where you are able to control your

own destiny, make as much money as you want, and have a lot of fun doing it.

In regards to controlling your own destiny and making a ton of money, are you doing everything on a daily basis to hit those goals and striving to be the best?

In my opinion, this business is a lot about will power and not falling into the trap of laziness. After reading this book, I hope you know what you should be doing every call, appointment, day, week, month, year but how many of you are you doing that EVERY single call, appointment, day, week, month, year?

A few processes to consider:

- ▶ How many new businesses are you bringing to the table each week? 15-20?
  - ▷ Business prospecting should be done during non-money hours so you can spend the money hours capitalizing on the opportunities.
- ▶ How many times per day do you ask for an appointment? How many times per day do you ask the same person several times for an appointment?
- ▶ Are you proposing a package on every single appointment AND coming up with a definitive next step?
- ▶ How many times are you asking about cross-selling opportunities per day?
  - ▷ As soon as someone purchases a season ticket package, your next question should be planning out a group outing for them. Do not just ask if they want to do a group, get into

the conversation of planning out a specific group; what month, what day of the week, what game, what seating category? For Example: *"Welcome to the family, we are looking forward to having you on board for the season. I also can help you put together a perfect group outing with you and your friends, what month and day of the week would be a great opportunity for you and all of your friends to come out a game together?"*

- ► How many times are you asking for referrals on every call?
  - ▷ Don't just stop at "Who do you know?"

When you look back at your sales career, do you want to be known as the person that is #1 in your department, #1 in the organization, or the **best salesperson in the professional sports industry?**

You have a great opportunity in front of us, you need to make sure you are giving it your all EVERY single day and striving to be the best!!!

Cal Ripken, Jr. was my favorite player as I previously mentioned in my I/My statement. When I played sports, I always wore number 8 as I always looked up to his work ethic, leadership, and focus every single day. With the book coming to a close, I am going to leave each of you with 8 key take-a-ways. Like I mentioned before, I hope you can come back and read specific chapters and apply something to your day to day.

1. Passion, Work Ethic, Coachability Every Day.

2. Go above and beyond the call of duty.
3. Put yourself in a position to be successful.
4. Surround yourself with good people.
5. Be a sponge.
6. Focus on improving every day.
7. Bounce back from struggles.
8. HAVE FUN!!!

ACKNOWLEDGMENTS

Writing a book is harder than I thought and more reward-ing than I could have ever imagined. None of this would have been possible without my family and friends. They have continued to challenge me, keep me motivated, stood by me during struggles, and most importantly helped me continue to hustle.

A special thanks to the people that have hired and de-veloped me along the way. Corey Breton, who took a chance on a kid from Ohio with limited sales skills. Bernie Mul-lin, Lou DePaoli, Brendan Donohue, and Chris Zaber who continued to put a blueprint in front of me to be successful and helped me get my first and many leadership roles. To Charlie Freeman, Michael Forde, and Chris D'Orso for teaching me a new way of leadership. Nic Barlage for hav-ing the confidence in hiring me to lead an entire team at a young age. Amy Brooks for putting a role together to show my skillset in front of the entire NBA family. Derek Jeter and Chip Bowers for giving me an opportunity to rebuild with a new ownership and leadership team.

Thank you to all of the team members that I have been fortunate enough to hire, train, and develop. It's been a pleasure watching each of you grow and evolve on your own.

Thank you to my editor, Dan Crissman, in really getting the context to flow, and to Stewart Williams with the design help to make the book stand out.

I could certainly go on forever about the additional leaders and team members that have helped me along the way in my career and personal life and will continue to do, so thank you!

My life and career has been a fun journey and I hope you enjoyed the book and hope you can create a remarkable path for yourself.

ABOUT THE AUTHOR

TRAVIS APPLE works for General Sports Worldwide in the Worldwide Executive Search and Consulting Division that he and Lou DePaoli created. The vertical is comprised of multiple different layers ranging from recruiting, onboarding, training, development, business planning, consulting, and much more. Prior to starting this business, Travis was the Vice President of Ticket Sales & Service for both the Miami Marlins and the Phoenix Suns as well as working at the NBA League Office in Team Marketing and Business Operations. Travis has also spent time with the Orlando Magic, Pittsburgh Pirates, and Atlanta Hawks and Thrashers.

He hosts a weekly podcast "52 Weeks of Hustle" where he has conversations with top ranking professionals in the sports industry.

Travis is a native of Delphos, Ohio, and attended Ashland University where he tripled majored in Sports Communication, Journalism, and Electronic Media Production.